American Monsters

Volume Five

12 Terrifying Tales of America's Most Depraved Serial Killers

Robert Keller

Please Leave Your Review of This Book At
http://bit.ly/kellerbooks

ISBN-13: 978-1535162272

ISBN-10: 1535162279

© 2016 by Robert Keller

robertkellerauthor.com

All rights reserved.

No part of this publication may be copied or reproduced in any format, electronic or otherwise, without the prior, written consent of the copyright holder and publisher. This book is for informational and entertainment purposes only and the author and publisher will not be held responsible for the misuse of information contain herein, whether deliberate or incidental.

Much research, from a variety of sources, has gone into the compilation of this material. To the best knowledge of the author and publisher, the material contained herein is factually correct. Neither the publisher, nor author will be held responsible for any inaccuracies.

Table of Contents

Coral Eugene Watts 5

Harvey Robinson 15

Albert De Salvo 25

Angel Resendiz 39

Dean Corll 47

Nannie Doss 63

Gary Ray Bowles 75

Edmund Kemper 83

Charles Albright 93

Carl Panzram 101

Loren Herzog & Wesley Shermantine Jr. 111

Randy Kraft 119

What Makes A Serial Killer? 129

Coral Eugene Watts

The Sunday Morning Slasher

*"She had evil eyes. I was trying to release her spirit." –
Coral Watts*

In May 1982, Lori Lister, 21, arrived at her apartment in Houston, Texas after visiting her boyfriend. As she parked her car and walked towards the front door of her building, she was probably unaware that she was being followed. But a man was tracking her, and as she slotted her key into the front door, he came up quickly behind her and put his hands on her neck. Lori's screams were quickly cut off as the man increased pressure on her throat. She felt the light fading, she was sure that she was going to die.

Fortunately for Lori, her muffled cries had been heard by a neighbor, who was on the phone to the police, even as the attacker dragged Lori inside. As the man eased Lori to the floor, he encountered her roommate, 18-year-old Melinda Aguilar. He threatened to slash Melinda's throat if she screamed, then choked her into submission. Fearing for her life, Melinda decided to play dead. It worked. The attacker lowered her to the carpet and then began binding the girls' hands with coat hangers. That completed, he did a peculiar thing. He was so excited to have control over the two women that he jumped up and down, clapping his hands like some fairy tale ogre. He then walked to the bathroom and began filling the tub.

Melinda waited until he was out of sight, then staggered to her feet and crossed the room to the second-floor balcony. She clambered over the railing and dropped to the ground, screaming for all she was worth, hoping it wasn't too late to save her friend's life. Moments later, a police car screeched to a halt outside the building.

Hearing the sirens, the intruder tried to flee but the police officers cut off his escape and apprehended him in the courtyard. Meanwhile, the neighbor who had called the police rushed to Lori and Melissa's apartment. He was just in time to pull Lori from the tub, where the intruder had been trying to drown her.

Investigators soon identified the attacker as Coral Eugene Watts. Asked why he had tried to kill the women, Watts said that they had "evil eyes" and that he was trying to "release their spirits." He also told officers that he had done it before – at least 80 times.

Carl Eugene Watts was born on November 7, 1953, in Killeen, Texas. His father, Richard, was a soldier, based at Fort Hood at the time of Carl's birth. His mother, Dorothy Mae, was a teacher. Just days after Carl was born, the couple moved back to their hometown of Coalwood, West Virginia. A year later their second child, Sharon, was born.

Richard and Dorothy Mae had been childhood sweethearts, but their marriage was an unhappy one that eventually ended in divorce in 1955. Following the breakup, Dorothy Mae moved with her two children to Inkster, Michigan, where she found work as a high school art teacher. But the family would regularly return to Coalwood to visit relatives, and Carl loved the southern town so much that he later changed his name to Coral - a southern pronunciation of his name.

In 1962, Coral's mother re-married, a situation that greatly distressed the boy, partly because he didn't like his new stepfather and partly because he hated having a competitor for his mother's affections.

Around this time, another life-changing event occurred in his life. He developed meningitis, his temperature running so high that doctors feared it might have caused brain damage. Coral recovered, but it seemed that the doctors' assessment had been right. There were changes to his behavior, subtle at first, but plain to see for all who knew him.

The first sign was in his academic performance. Coral had missed a year of school due to his illness and was held back a grade when he returned. But the formerly bright student had difficulty concentrating and his grades began to slip, leaving his mother to wonder how badly his illness had affected him.

Then there were the dreams, violent dramas in which he tussled with the evil spirits of women and killed them. More worrying was his assessment of these nightmares. They didn't frighten him, the young boy declared, in fact, he enjoyed them.

If his parents took this as a warning sign as to the state of his mental health they appear to have taken no action until, inevitably, his fantasies manifested in reality. In 1968, when Coral was 15, he knocked on the door of a 26-year-old woman named Joan Gave.

When Mrs. Gave answered the door, Coral forced her back into her apartment, pushed her to the floor, and started beating her. When he was done, he left her apartment and continued his newspaper delivery route as if nothing had happened.

Gave immediately called the police, and they were waiting for Coral when he returned home. Brought before a judge, he was ordered to undergo psychiatric treatment at the Lafayette Clinic in Detroit. Here, psychiatrists diagnosed him with strong homicidal tendencies and flagged him as a danger to others. Nonetheless, the boy was released just a few months later, on his 16th birthday.

He was ordered to undergo outpatient treatment, which amounted to just nine subsequent consultations.

Coral returned to school, where his academic performance remained poor. He excelled, though, at sports, particularly football and boxing, which allowed him to release his pent-up aggression.

With extensive tutoring by his mother, he graduated high school at age 19, and despite his low grade point average, he won a football scholarship to Lane College in Jackson, Tennessee. However, he remained at school only a few months before returning home. He said that it was due to a leg injury that prevented him from playing football. More likely, he just couldn't bear to be away from his mother.

Back in Michigan, Watts found work as an apprentice mechanic in Detroit, remaining at that trade for a year before enrolling at Western Michigan University in Kalamazoo. Soon after, there was a rash of attacks in the area around the campus - one of them fatal.

On October 25, 1974, Lenore Knizacky, 23, heard a knock at her front door. When she answered it, a young black man was standing there. He said he was looking for someone named Charles, but before she could answer he grabbed her by the throat and forced her into the apartment. He began strangling her, but she managed to fight him off, forcing him to flee.

Five days later, on October 30, 19-year-old Gloria Steele opened her door to a man who said he was looking for Charles. The man forced his way in and attacked Gloria with a knife, stabbing her 33 times.

The man tried the same ruse with another student on November 12. Fortunately, she was able to escape and as the man fled the scene and jumped into his vehicle, she noted down his license plate number. Police followed up. The car belonged to Coral Eugene Watts.

Watts was soon in custody on two charges of battery and he readily admitted the charges, even adding that he'd attacked at least a dozen more women. He balked though when confronted with the murder of Gloria Steele, insisting that he hadn't killed anyone.

As a precursor to his court hearing, Watts was ordered to undergo a psychiatric evaluation at Kalamazoo State Hospital. Psychiatrists there found that he was emotionally detached and lacked remorse for his actions. They diagnosed him with an antisocial personality disorder but insisted that he was well aware of the difference between right and wrong and, therefore, competent to stand trial.

Watts would spend six months under psychiatric care during which time he suffered from depression and made a half-hearted attempt at suicide. When his case eventually came to trial in the summer of 1975, he was sentenced to a year in jail on the battery charges. Unfortunately, he was never charged with the murder of

Gloria Steele because prosecutors lacked the evidence to convict him. If they had, an awful lot of lives might have been saved.

After Watts was released in 1976, he found work as a mechanic and returned to live with his mother. Those who knew him described him as a "mama's boy" because he didn't like being away from his mother. The other women in his life just didn't measure up.

But that is not to say that there weren't other women. Shortly after his release from prison, Watts began seeing a woman named Delores, fathering a child by her before they split. He then started dating another woman, Valeria, who he married in 1979. The marriage lasted just six months before Valeria walked out, mainly due to Coral's bizarre conduct.

Years later, Valeria would describe some of his behaviors to investigators. She said that he suffered violent nightmares, would throw garbage on the floor, would slash at houseplants with a knife, and melt candles into the furniture. She also said that, immediately after they had sex, Watts would leave the house and stay away for several hours.

Watts never explained where he went on these occasions, but investigators were able to provide a ready explanation. They believed that Watts was out stalking victims. Several women were attacked and murdered during this period, in attacks bearing Watts' unique signature.

One of those attacks occurred on Halloween 1979. Detroit News reporter Jeanne Clyne, 44, was attacked as she walked home from a doctor's appointment. She died from 11 stab wounds, inflicted on a busy suburban road, in broad daylight.

Then, on April 20, high school student Shirley Small was killed by two knife wounds to the heart, outside her home in Ann Arbor, Michigan. Another Ann Arbor woman perished in a similar attack. Glenda Richmond, 26, was stabbed 28 times, outside the diner that she managed. An even more frenzied attack occurred on September 14. University of Michigan graduate student, Rebecca Huff, 20, suffered at least 50 knife wounds.

In the wake of the Huff murder, a task force was formed to investigate the recent spate of homicides in the area. Under the leadership of Detective Paul Bunten, the task force soon identified Watts as a suspect and brought him in on a warrant to provide a blood sample. Bunten had hoped that he might coax a confession out of Watts, but Watts wasn't talking. Neither did the blood sample connect him to any crime.

Annoyed by the police attention, Watts decided to leave town, relocating to Columbus, Texas, where he found work at an oil company. Columbus is just 70 miles from Houston. Soon Coral Watts took to cruising that city, looking for new victims.

But Paul Bunten wasn't about to let Watts off the hook that easily. As soon as he heard about the move, he contacted the Houston police to warn them about the serial killer who had just arrived in their city. He even sent them copies of his files on Watts, in the hope of preventing more murders.

Houston PD, however, had been unable to locate Watts, and the warning from Bunten was soon forgotten. It would remain so until the attack on Lori Lister and Melinda Aguilar in May 1982. Now under arrest for those crimes, Watts clammed up and refused to talk. His refusal drove Harris County Assistant District Attorney Ira Jones, to offer an extraordinary deal. He promised Watts immunity on any murder charges he confessed to.

One of America's most horrendous serial killers had just been given the equivalent of a get-out-of-jail-free card, and unsurprisingly, Watts took the deal. On August 9, 1982, he confessed to 13 murders. He hinted that he might have been the man responsible for the 1979 Detroit murder of Jeanne Clyne but insisted that he hadn't killed Glenda Richard, Shirley Small, or Rebecca Huff (even though there was strong physical and circumstantial evidence linking him to those crimes). As to his Houston victims, he confessed to drowning University of Texas student Linda Tilley, 22, in her apartment complex swimming pool in September 1981. He also admitted to stabbing 25-year-old Elizabeth Montgomery to death, one week later.

The same day, he killed Susan Wolf, 21, stabbing her to death as she returned from the grocery store. In January 1982, he strangled 27-year-old Phyllis Tamm, while she was out jogging. Two days later, he murdered architecture student Margaret Fossi, 25. Her body was later found in the trunk of her car at Rice University.

During that month, Watts attacked three more Houston women, slashing one across the throat, stabbing one with a knife and another with an ice pick. Miraculously, all three survived.

His next victims were not as lucky. Between February and May 1982, Watts killed Elena Semander, 20; Emily LaQua, 14; Anna Ledet, 34; Yolanda Gracia, 21; Carrie Jefferson, 32; Suzanne Searles, 25, and Michele Maday, 20.

He admitted to at least 80 more murders in Michigan and Canada but refused to give any details because his immunity deal only applied to the murders committed in Texas.

Eventually brought to trial for the attack on Lori Lister and Melinda Aguilar, Watts pled guilty to one count of burglary with intent to kill, the plea bargain he'd agreed to. He was sentenced to 60 years in prison, parting with these chilling words, "You know, if they ever let me out, I'll kill again."

And Watts may well have had the opportunity to make good on his threat. In 1989, the Texas Court of Criminal Appeals ruled that the judge had failed to inform Watts that the bathtub he'd attempted to drown Lori Lister in was construed as a lethal weapon. Consequently, he was now considered a "non-violent" inmate and would not be required to serve his full term. The man who had sworn that he would kill again if he ever got out, was due for mandatory parole on May 9, 2006.

It was a terrifying thought and as the date grew closer, authorities in Michigan and Texas were desperate for any reason to keep Coral Watts behind bars. They began revisiting old cases, searching for evidence that might have been overlooked, evidence that might be used to keep Coral Watts off the streets. They eventually found it in the 1979 murder of Helen Mae Dutcher.

Dutcher had been attacked in an alleyway outside a Ferndale, Michigan, dry cleaning establishment and had been stabbed 12 times in the neck and back. An eyewitness, Joseph Foy, had reported the murder, but the police hadn't been able to catch the attacker, even though the composite gleaned from Foy's description strongly resembled Watts.

In 2004, Foy saw a television program regarding the Watts case and again contacted the police. It was the break investigators had been waiting for. With an eyewitness to the murder, they filed new charges against Watts.

Coral Watts was extradited to Michigan in April 2004. His trial began in November and ended with a guilty verdict for first-degree murder. Because Michigan doesn't have the death penalty, Watts was sentenced to life imprisonment without the possibility of parole. He died in prison on Friday, September 21, 2007, of prostate cancer. He was 53 years old.

Harvey Robinson

Charlotte Schmoyer delivered the Morning Call newspaper to an area centered on East Gordon Street, Allentown, Pennsylvania. Usually, the 15-year-old was diligent in her work, but on the morning of June 9, 1993, she was late, which somewhat annoyed one of her customers. The customer looked out of her window hoping to spot Charlotte but saw instead her delivery cart abandoned in the street. Thinking this was suspicious, she called the police.

After ascertaining with Charlotte's supervisor that she hadn't returned to the depot, a unit was dispatched to the scene. What they found there gave them cause for concern, the girl's bicycle lying on its side, her portable radio smashed on the floor.

A few hours later, police received an anonymous tip, which sent them to a wooded area near the East Side Reservoir. There they found a trail of blood leading from the parking lot into the trees, as well as a discarded sneaker. A brief search turned up Charlotte's body, lying in the woods, covered with leaves. An autopsy would later reveal that she'd been raped, then stabbed 22 times in the back and neck before her throat was slashed. Police turned up some vital clues in processing the scene, a pubic hair on the girl's sweatshirt, and a head hair on her knee.

But those clues led nowhere, and neither did witness reports of a light blue car seen in the area at the time of the attack. Residents and police worried that the killer might strike again. Little did they know that Charlotte Schmoyer was actually his second victim, that he'd killed 8 months before and had only waited this long to kill again because he'd been incarcerated in a juvenile detention center.

The first attack occurred on August 9, 1992. Joan Burghardt was a 29-year-old who suffered from a mental illness and required assisted living. A couple of days before, Joan had reported to her parents that someone had tried to break into her apartment by cutting through a screen door. Now, two days later, she was unaware that the same man had followed her home, and was watching her. As she entered the living room, the man suddenly burst through a window and came at her. He struck her so hard that her blood splattered the wall.

But despite her injury, Joan managed to run past him into another room, where she banged on the wall and screamed for all she was worth. Turning on the television to mask her screams the killer came after her. He caught her in the bedroom and delivered 37 brutal blows to her head with a blunt instrument, fracturing her skull. When he was sure she was dead, he masturbated over her body and then raped her. Then, despite being drenched in Joan

Burghardt's blood, he walked casually across a field, to his home four blocks away. Several residents of Joan's building would later testify to having heard her desperate screams. No one had come to her aid.

Not long after he murdered Joan Burghardt, the killer had been locked up on an unrelated charge. Upon his release, he'd gone to revisit the scene of his crime. It had been then that he'd spotted Charlotte Schmoyer. Now he was hunting again and he soon came across a woman who took his fancy, tall and buxom, like he preferred.

Thirty-seven-year-old, Denise Sam-Cali ran a limousine and bus service with her husband John. Living just a mile from their business premises on the east side of the city, it was her daily habit to walk to and from work. On one of these walks, the killer spotted her and followed. Over the next few days, he learned her routine and where she lived. Then he waited.

On June 17, Denise and John Sam-Cali returned from a short trip to find that their house had been broken into. Entering with trepidation, they were surprised to find that, but for a few moved items, the house seemed undisturbed. Upstairs, though, it was another story, John's gun collection, which he'd kept in a closet, was gone. He immediately phoned the police.

The break-in disturbed the Sam-Cali's. Not only had their home been violated but John was left with a feeling of trepidation. What if the burglar had arrived when they were in the house? What if he'd caught him and Denise sleeping? What if...? He pushed those thoughts from his mind. Those things hadn't happened. All he could do was ensure that he and his wife were protected if an attack did happen. He purchased another couple of firearms. He also started to teach his wife how to shoot.

The killer meanwhile, had been active. While Denise Sam-Cali had been out of town, he'd been tracking another potential victim. On June 20, he broke into her house, snuck up the stairs, and peered into her bedroom. To his frustration, he saw that she was not alone. Her boyfriend had stayed over. Still, his blood was up, for a brief moment he considered attacking the two of them, but he decided against it. The man looked big. It was too much of a risk.

Anger and frustration boiling inside him, he crept through the house and found another bedroom where the woman's five-year-old daughter lay asleep. He moved quickly, cutting off the child's cries and then choking her into unconsciousness and carrying her downstairs. In the laundry room, he raped the little girl, then throttled her, tossing her body aside when he was done. Then he left and walked to his home, just two blocks away.

Miraculously, the victim of his attack was not dead. In the early morning hours, she regained consciousness and dragged herself to her mother's room. Her mother called the police. Later, a doctor would confirm that she'd been savagely choked and sexually attacked.

The attack on the little girl had left the killer frustrated. She was not what he wanted, not his preferred victim type. Then, when he read in the papers that she'd survived the attack, he became afraid. What if she'd seen his face, what if she knew who he was, what if she saw him on the street and recognized him? He lay low for a week, half expecting the police to knock on his door at any time. When that didn't happen, he went out again and started tracking his original target, Denise Sam-Cali.

On June 28, 1993, Denise was home alone, John having gone out of town on a business trip. On that evening, she visited with an aunt who lived on the same street and came home late. She was carrying her gun, but still she felt nervous, two violent attacks on females in the past month, plus the break-in to her residence, had her jumpy. She went quickly inside, checked doors and windows, and then undressed and got into bed.

But, she couldn't sleep. She lay awake, anxious, listening to her heartbeat, listening to the sounds of the night, every one of them sounding like a potential threat. Suddenly, her breath caught in her throat. She'd heard something. Something that sounded like it had come from inside the house, a noise like crackling paper.

She sat up in bed, heart pounding. "Who's there?" she called out in the time-honored fashion of every horror movie heroine. Nothing, not a sound. But the silence was telling, she knew she was not alone. Suddenly, she wanted badly to be out of the house.

She slid out of bed, slipped into a nightgown, and edged towards the door. She peered into the hall and saw only blackness, then braced herself and ran for the front door. As she did, a figure separated itself from the dark, a wicked-looking knife in his hand. Denise raced away from him, made it to the front door, and started working at the locks. As she did, she felt his hand close on her arm and spin her around. He slashed at her, opening her lip, and she struck out at him desperately, clattering the blade from his hand. As he tried to retrieve it, she finally threw the door open and sprinted out into the front yard.

The man caught her on the lawn, grabbing her by the hair and throwing her to the ground. He pinned her to the ground and began to work at the button of his pants while he throttled her one-handed. She tried to scream but achieved nothing more than a gurgle. That was enough for him to make him punch her, once, twice, three, four times in the face, hefty blows. Then he increased the pressure on her throat, choking her until she passed out.

Denise Sam-Cali would have died right there on her front lawn if a neighbor hadn't heard the commotion and turned on an outside floodlight, which scared the attacker off. Denise managed to crawl inside and call 911. Later, doctors assessed her injuries. The lip was going to require plastic surgery, and her face and neck were badly bruised. Denise wasn't sure if she had been raped (tests would later prove that she had been), but she was lucky to be alive.

When John Sam-Cali returned from his business trip, he was shocked to learn what had happened. He immediately had a burglar alarm installed but insisted that his wife stay with relatives while she recovered from her traumatic experience. Denise was able to provide a description of her attacker, who she said was a young white man, about five-foot-seven, muscular, and clean-shaven.

Police were afraid that the man might return to try and silence Denise if he believed she could identify him and that belief was vindicated on the night of July 18. Fortunately, the Sam-Cali's newly fitted alarm scared the intruder off, but in the morning they realized that several items, including a .38 revolver, were missing.

Acting in the belief that the intruder might try again, police came up with an idea. One that might put the Sam-Cali's at risk, but which might also allow them to catch the attacker. They proposed that the couple should stay in their home to lure the killer, while an officer hid in the house to apprehend him if he showed up. The brave couple readily agreed.

The killer meanwhile had been stalking another victim, just a mile from where the Sam-Calis lived. Jessica Jean Fortney, 47, lived with her daughter and son-in-law, and their seven-year-old daughter. On July 14, the killer broke in and attacked Jessica, bludgeoning and raping her and then, strangling her to death before making his escape. But there'd been a witness. Jessica's 7-year-old granddaughter had seen the entire attack from her bedroom. Her description suggested that the killer was the same man who'd attacked Denise Sam-Cali.

The last murder had sated him, but the killer remained driven by an obsession. One woman had escaped his clutches and he still wanted her. On July 31, he returned to the Sam-Cali residence.

At around 1:30, Officer Brian Lewis, on duty inside the house, heard a noise, someone was trying to pry open the patio door. A while later, a gloved hand reached through a living room window and removed the screen. Officer Lewis pressed a button on his handset, summoning support. Then he crouched in the darkness and waited for the killer to enter. In the next moment, the window eased open and a short, muscular man dressed entirely in black climbed through.

"Halt! Police!" Lewis shouted as he rose to show himself. But the man didn't stop. He sprinted towards the kitchen and reached for a gun in his waistband. Lewis fired at him and the man fired back. Then, as Lewis was reloading, he heard the intruder banging against the kitchen door trying to escape. Lewis ran for the Sam-Cali's bedroom and told them to stay put. Then he edged back into the darkness and made his way towards the kitchen.

Backup had arrived by now, and officers were surrounding the house, but as Lewis entered the kitchen, he saw that the intruder had escaped by smashing his way through a glass door. He'd cut himself in the process, though; there was a copious amount of blood on the floor, trailing out into the yard. Lewis also thought that one of his bullets might have found its mark.

The police quickly alerted all hospitals in the area, asking them to report anyone coming in with serious cuts or a bullet wound. It paid off. At around 5:30 a.m., a young man walked into the ER at Lehigh Valley Hospital with serious cuts to his arm and leg. He was immediately arrested. His name was Harvey Miguel Robinson, and he lived on the East Side, close to the sites of all the attacks. He was just 18 years old.

Robinson was arraigned on multiple charges, with bail set at $1 million. Even as he continued to protest his innocence he was brought to trial on July 24, 1994. On November 8, he was found guilty of the rapes and murders of Joan Burghardt, Charlotte Schmoyer, and Jessica Fortney. Two days later the jury delivered a death sentence for each of the murders.

The death penalties in the cases of Burghardt and Schmoyer were later vacated on appeal, but in December 2005, the Pennsylvania Supreme Court affirmed the death sentence for the murder of Jessica Fortney.

Harvey Robinson awaits his date with the executioner on Pennsylvania's death row, at Graterford.

Albert De Salvo

The Boston Strangler

It is one of the most infamous serial killer cases in U.S. history, the first case extensively covered by mass-market television, radio, and the national press, a case that sparked widespread panic in the city of Boston, a case that continues to fascinate, even to this day.

Between June 1962 and January 1964, 13 Massachusetts women fell victim to a serial killer, a fiend who has gone down in history by the notorious epithet, the Boston Strangler. The killer entered the homes of his victims without force, apparently talking his way in. Once inside, he sexually molested the women before strangling them with articles of clothing and fleeing the scene. Many of the victims were posed, others had sexually degrading post-mortem acts performed upon them, all were killed in their own homes.

Albert De Salvo, a hyper-sexed factory worker, sex offender, and petty criminal, confessed to the crimes, and although he was never officially charged with the murders, he entered the public consciousness as the Strangler, a belief that held for decades. Yet there is significant evidence to suggest that De Salvo was not the killer. Indeed, many of the detectives working the case believed that the murders were not the work of a single man but of two, and possibly more, perpetrators, working independently.

The first murder occurred on June 14, 1962. Anna Slesers, a 55-year-old divorcee living in the Back Bay area was due to attend a memorial service that evening and had arranged for her son, Juris, to pick her up at 7 o'clock. However, when Juris arrived at his mother's apartment, there was no reply.

At first, Juris was annoyed, then concerned, when his pounding on the door brought no response. Eventually, he applied his shoulder to the door and forced it open. His worst fears were confirmed as he walked through the apartment and saw his mother lying on the bathroom floor with the cord from her robe wound tightly around her neck.

Responding to the call, detectives James Mellon and John Driscoll found the petite woman provocatively displayed, the cloth cord of her housecoat knotted around her neck, and tied in a decorative bow. The apartment appeared to have been ransacked, although a gold watch and several pieces of jewelry, left out in the open, had not been taken.

Just a couple of weeks later, on June 30, there was another murder. Nina Nichols lived alone in an apartment in the Brighton area of Boston. The 68-year-old, retired physiotherapist was found sexually assaulted and strangled with a pair of nylon stockings, the ends knotted in a bow. As with the Slesers murder, Nina Nichols' body had been posed and the apartment ransacked, although none of her valuables had been taken.

That same day, in the suburb of Lynn, some 15 miles north of Boston, an almost identical murder was committed. Helen Blake, a 65-year-old divorcee, was raped, and then strangled with a stocking, her body left suggestively posed. Her apartment had been thoroughly ransacked, but although two diamond rings were missing, other valuables were left untouched.

This latest murder set alarm bells jangling at police headquarters. Three homicides in a relatively small area, over a period of just two weeks, all of them bearing a clear signature, and quite possibly committed by the same man. As Police Commissioner Edmund McNamara canceled all police leave and put detectives on the ground checking on known sex offenders, a warning went out via the media to Boston's women. They were advised to keep doors locked and to be wary of admitting strangers to their homes.

These measures didn't deter the Strangler at all. On August 21, 75-year-old, Ida Irga, was found dead in her apartment. The shy, retiring widow had been strangled with a pillowcase, her nude body posed flat on its back, each ankle resting on a chair, the placement (facing the door) designed for maximum shock value. She'd been dead two days by the time she was found.

Just 24 hours later, came another grisly discovery. Jane Sullivan, a 67-year-old nurse, lived across town from Ida Irga, in Dorchester. She had been dead for 10 days before her body was found, laid out in her bathtub. The condition of the corpse made it impossible to determine whether she'd been sexually assaulted or not.

As panic gripped the city of Boston, there was a three-month reprieve before the next murder. This crime, however, was somewhat different. Up until now, the Strangler had targeted older victims, but Sophie Clark, an attractive, African-American student, was just 21 years old. On December 5, 1962, Sophie's roommates returned home to find her nude body, lying legs apart, three nylon stockings knotted tightly around her neck. She'd been sexually assaulted and there was semen found on the rug close to her body.

There was no sign of forced entry which Sophie's roommates thought was strange. They assured the detectives that Sophie had been extremely security conscious, insisting on an extra lock on the door and even questioning friends before admitting them to the apartment.

As police questioned the neighbors, an interesting lead turned up. Mrs. Marcella Lulka told officers that around 2:20 that afternoon a man had knocked on her door and said that the building manager had sent him to speak to her about painting her apartment. He'd then complimented her on her figure, and asked if she'd ever thought of modeling.

Mrs. Lulka had asked the man to be quiet, by raising a finger to her lips. She'd told him that her husband was asleep in the next room and he'd then said it was the wrong apartment and hurried away. The man was 25 to 30 years old, she said, of average height with honey-colored hair. He'd been wearing a dark jacket and dark green trousers.

A check with the building manager revealed that he hadn't engaged anyone to do any painting, leading police to suspect that this man was the Strangler, especially as Sophie Clark was killed at around 2:30 in the afternoon. Why, though, had the security-conscious Sophie let him in?

Three weeks after the murder of Sophie Clark, a 23-year-old secretary named Patricia Bissette failed to show up for work. Her boss was concerned about her, so he called on her apartment. Getting no response when he knocked, he tracked down the building superintendent and the two of them entered the apartment through a window.

They found Patricia Bissette lying face up in bed, the covers drawn up to her chin. Several stockings were knotted around her neck. The medical examiner would later confirm that she'd been raped and possibly sodomized.

On Wednesday, May 8, 1963, friends of Beverly Samans, a 23-year-old graduate student, became concerned when she didn't show up for choir practice at the Second Unitarian Church in Back Bay. A friend went to her apartment to check on Beverley, entering with a key that she had given him. As the man opened the front door, a shocking scene awaited him. Beverley's nude body lay in plain view, her legs splayed, a nylon stocking, and two handkerchiefs woven together and knotted around her neck. The cause of death wasn't strangulation, though, she'd been stabbed 22 times.

The summer of 1963 brought another break in the killings. Then, on September 8, 1963, a 58-year-old divorcee, named Evelyn Corbin, was found strangled in her home in Salem, Massachusetts. Two nylon stockings were knotted around her neck and her panties were stuffed into her mouth as a gag. Her apartment had been ransacked but valuables lying in plain sight hadn't been taken.

On November 25, while Bostonians joined the rest of the country in grieving the death of assassinated President John F. Kennedy, another murder occurred. Joann Graff was a 23-year-old industrial designer. She'd been dead three days by the time her body was found with two nylon stockings tied in an elaborate bow around her neck. There were teeth marks on her breast and there was evidence that she'd been sexually assaulted.

As detectives questioned other residents in the building, they uncovered a clue that provided a link to the Sophie Clark case. A student who lived in the apartment above Joann reported that, at around 3:25 p.m. on the day of the murder, a stranger had knocked on his door. The man was about mid-twenties with elaborately pomaded hair, dressed in dark green slacks and a dark shirt and jacket. The man asked if Joann Graff lived there (pronouncing her name incorrectly as "Joan"). The student had said no and directed the man to the correct apartment. A moment later he heard knocking from the floor below and then a door opening and closing. When a friend of Joann's phoned her 10 minutes later, there was no reply.

Just over a month later on January 4, 1964, two young women returned home to a gruesome discovery. Their roommate, 19-year-old Mary Sullivan, lay murdered, displayed in a shocking fashion. She was posed, sitting upright on a bed. Two stockings and a pink silk scarf were knotted around her neck, and a "Happy New Year" card rested against her feet. A thick liquid that looked like semen was dripping from her mouth onto her breasts. A broomstick handle had been rammed into her vagina.

The brutal murder of Mary Sullivan and the disrespectful way in which she had been posed was the last straw for Massachusetts Attorney General Edward Brooke. On January 17, 1964, he announced that he was personally taking charge of the case. In short order, Brooke ordered the formation of a task force, formally called the Special Division of Crime Research and Detection. He placed Assistant Attorney General John S. Bottomly in charge of the team, a controversial choice as Bottomly had no experience of criminal law and was universally disliked by the senior hierarchy of the Boston Police Department.

And Bottomly's first action hardly improved his standing with his police colleagues. He brought in Peter Hurkos, a controversial Dutch psychic who seemed to make a habit of involving himself in high-profile murder investigations. Hurkos had achieved some limited measure of success in the past, most notably in the Melvin Rees case, but he failed woefully in identifying the Boston Strangler. The suspect he named could be categorically cleared of involvement in any of the murders. It was a blow to Hurkos' credibility and to that of the task force.

At this point in the story, it is necessary to make a small detour, to a bizarre series of sex offenses that occurred in the Cambridge area a couple of years before the Boston Strangler appeared on the scene. Over a period of three months, a man in his late twenties took to knocking on doors and introducing himself as the representative of a modeling agency. He'd tell any woman who answered that she'd been recommended to the agency, and ask if he could measure her to ascertain that she met the agency's requirements. Many of the women, flattered by the attention and interested in the money he said they could earn, allowed him to take their measurements. That done, he'd thank them, and say he'd be in touch. Of course, they never heard from him again and most of the women put it down as a harmless prank. Others, though, were offended and reported the matter to the police.

On March 17, 1961, Cambridge police apprehended a man trying to break into a house. Under questioning, the man confessed to being the "Measuring Man." He was Albert De Salvo, a 29-year-old Bostonian with numerous arrests for breaking and entering. Asked what the point of his "Measuring Man" charade was, he said it was a prank to get one over smart, high-class people. Prank or not, De

Salvo's got 18 months. He was released in April 1962, two months before the first Boston Strangler murder.

In November of 1964, almost three years after his release from prison, and 11 months after the murder of Mary Sullivan, De Salvo was arrested again. This time, the charges were more serious. On October 27, he entered a residence and placed a knife to a woman's throat as she dozed. He tied her up and stuffed underwear in her mouth then stripped her naked and fondled her before fleeing the apartment. Before he left he apologized for what he'd done.

The woman had gotten a good look at her attacker and her description reminded the investigating officers of the Measuring Man. They brought De Salvo in, and the victim identified him from a lineup. A check with other jurisdictions turned up an interest from Connecticut. They'd had several similar attacks there and had given their unknown assailant the nickname, "The Green Man," because he always wore green work pants.

Faced with the accusations, De Salvo admitted to breaking into over 400 apartments and assaulting over 300 women. The police took these numbers with a pinch of salt. De Salvo was well known as a braggart with a habit of exaggerating. Nonetheless, he was in serious trouble.

De Salvo was sent to Bridgewater State Hospital for observation where his cellmate was a man named George Nassar, accused of the execution-style killing of a gas station attendant. Although he was a vicious killer, who'd previously served time for another murder, Nasser was an intelligent man. He possessed a near-genius IQ and spoke several languages. He was also known for his ability to manipulate, and at Bridgewater, he became Albert De Salvo's confidant. Not long after, Nasser placed a call to his attorney, F. Lee Bailey and Bailey took a flight from the West Coast to meet with De Salvo.

No one knows why Albert De Salvo confessed to being the Boston Strangler. It has been speculated that he and Nasser cooked up a scheme whereby De Salvo would confess and Nasser would turn him in and claim the reward money, which they'd later split. De Salvo expected to go to prison for life anyway, the money would go to his wife and two kids. Another theory is that the smooth-talking Nasser convinced De Salvo that there was a fortune to be made in book and movie rights. And it should also not be discounted that De Salvo was a braggart and a blowhard. The idea of being recognized as the infamous Boston Strangler must have appealed to him.

Whatever the motivation, F. Lee Bailey interviewed De Salvo at Bridgewater and then set up a meeting with Lieutenants Donovan and Sherry of the Strangler Task Force. At that meeting, he played them a tape of his interview with De Salvo, containing a confession to the Strangler murders. To the hard-pressed detectives of the Strangler task force, under increasing public and official scrutiny, De Salvo's confession must have been like manna from heaven. And there was no chance that it could be a fake. De Salvo's knowledge of the crime scenes was far too detailed, containing information that only the killer would know.

A meeting was hastily arranged between Police Commissioner McNamara, Dr. Ames Robey, the psychiatrist at Bridgewater, and De Salvo. This interview began on September 29, 1965, and resulted in more than 50 hours of tape and over 2000 pages of transcript. Again, De Salvo's detailed recollection of the crimes was impressive. Now, the police were faced with the arduous task of checking the details to make sure that De Salvo was telling the truth.

While they were doing that, De Salvo's attorney, F. Lee Bailey, sat down with Attorney General Brooke and John Bottomly, to thrash out a deal. Bailey came straight to the point. Despite De Salvo's confession, he did not believe that the State of Massachusetts had enough evidence to successfully try him as the Boston Strangler. However, De Salvo was prepared to plead guilty to the Green Man assaults and to accept a life sentence for those crimes.

Brook and Bottomly considered their options and decided that Bailey was right. Putting De Salvo on trial constituted a huge risk, as the court proceedings would fall right in the middle of Brook's election campaign for the Senate. A loss in court would seriously dent his chances. He thus agreed to Bailey's terms.

De Salvo went on trial for the Green Man charges on January 10, 1967, and was sentenced to life in prison. However, he would serve less than seven years of his sentence.

In November 1973, while in the infirmary at Walpole State Prison, Albert De Salvo was stabbed to death by an unknown assailant. The day before his death he had placed a call to Dr. Ames Robey. De Salvo was frantic, saying he had information to share on the Boston Strangler case and that he feared for his life. Dr. Robey agreed to meet with him the next morning, but De Salvo was murdered that night. His killer has never been caught.

So was Albert De Salvo the Boston Strangler? The evidence suggests that he was not. But if that is the case, it begs the question, how could he have had such intimate knowledge of the crime scenes?

The truth is that De Salvo got as much information wrong as he got right and that most of the so-called "intimate detail" he offered was public knowledge, having been reported in the papers. He did indeed provide some details that had been withheld from the public. But that information might easily have been fed to him, either by the real killer or by members of the Strangler task force, desperate to close the case.

Yet, even if we assume that De Salvo gained most of his knowledge by following the case in the newspapers, how could he, a man of below-average intelligence, memorize that much detail?

It turns out that De Salvo had a near photographic memory, as testified to by his lawyers Jon Asgeirsson and Tony Troy.

Then there's the issue of victim profiles. Serial killers most often target victims that are of similar type. Yet, in the Boston Strangler case, there are two distinct victim groups, one young, and one old. This seems to indicate two separate killers.

But might one of those killers not be De Salvo? Let's consider for a while the Green Man assaults, which started during the Boston Strangler's murderous campaign. Is it likely that Albert De Salvo could have been, simultaneously, a vicious murderer, and a man who tied up his victims, fondled them, and then fled the scene after apologizing for what he'd done? It seems highly unlikely.

All of the above is, of course, circumstantial, but there is physical evidence, too, that exonerates De Salvo, at least in one of the murders. For years, both the De Salvo and Sullivan families fought for the bodies of De Salvo and Mary Sullivan to be exhumed and for the evidence gathered from the scene to be put through DNA analysis. When this was eventually granted, in 2001, it proved two things; that Sullivan did not die in the way De Salvo described in his confession, and that whoever raped Mary Sullivan, wasn't Albert De Salvo.

Which leaves us with the question: Who was the Boston Strangler? In all likelihood, the Boston Strangler did not exist, at least not as the serial slayer of 13 women. The evidence suggests at least two killers, one targeting older women, one younger. Some of the murders might not even have been connected to either series.

As to who any of these men might have been, the best evidence we have are the eyewitness descriptions of the man seen near both the Clark and Graff murder scenes. Those eyewitnesses were brought to view De Salvo while he was incarcerated at Bridgewater. Both of them categorically said that De Salvo wasn't the man they'd seen. In fact, they said, the man more closely resembled De Salvo's cellmate, George Nasser.

Angel Resendiz

The Railroad Killer

For nearly two years, from August 1997 until July 1999, a brutal killer was at work in Texas, Kentucky, and Illinois. The fiend struck at will, attacking people who lived close to railway lines, strangling, shooting, and bludgeoning them to death in their homes, before disappearing without a trace. At first, investigators were baffled, but it soon became clear that the killer was riding the rails, stopping off where he chose to commit his atrocities, then making his escape by hopping the next freight train out of town. Following this line of inquiry would eventually lead investigators to Angel Maturino Resendiz a.k.a., The Railroad Killer.

Angel Resendiz was born in Izucar de Matamoros in the Mexican state of Puebla, on August 1, 1960. Not much is known about his childhood but it is believed that he was not raised by his biological family, but by another, who provided no guidance during his formative years. It is also believed that he may have been sexually abused as a child.

Virtually an orphan, Resendiz lived on the streets, surviving by begging, scavenging, and stealing. In this latter endeavor, he was soon lured by the richer pickings on the other side of the border in Texas. By his teens, he was making regular crossings.

Resendiz first came to the attention of the U.S. authorities in August 1976, when, at age 16, he was caught while trying to cross illegally into Brownsville, Texas. He was deported two months later but was soon back. INS agents apprehended him in Stirling Heights, Michigan in October, and a while later in McAllen, Texas. In 1988, he briefly lived in St. Louis where he worked part-time at a manufacturing company. He even managed to vote in two elections, using an assumed name.

His next run-in with the authorities was somewhat more serious than entering the country illegally. In September 1979, he was sentenced to 20 years in prison for auto theft and assault in Miami, Florida. Six years later, he was paroled and deported back to Mexico.

Resendiz would reappear on US soil several times over the next decade. In 1986, he served an 18-month prison term in Texas for falsely claiming citizenship. In 1988, he was arrested in New Orleans for carrying a concealed weapon. That same year he earned a 30-month sentence for trying to commit Social Security fraud in St. Louis. Then there was a bust for burglary in New Mexico in 1982, and a charge of trespassing and carrying a firearm in 1985.

After each of these infractions, he found himself put on a bus and shipped back to Mexico, but international borders meant little to Angel Resendiz. Often he'd be back in the United States within the day. Yet with each deportation, he became more and more angry, and over time that anger was directed, not just at the authorities, but at the whole population, they who had everything, while he was forced to scrape and scrounge for a living. Soon that anger would explode, and the petty crimes that had seen him shipped back and forth across the border for over two decades would morph into something considerably more serious – they'd morph into serial murder.

Resendiz had, in fact, been killing for some time before the two-year spree that brought him to the attention of the authorities. He claimed to have killed at least eight people in Mexico, but he was active in the US too.

His first known homicide in the US was the 1986 murder of an unidentified homeless woman. Resendiz said that he met her at a shelter and they took a motorcycle trip together. But the woman disrespected him, he said, so he shot her four times with a .38-caliber weapon and left her body at an abandoned farmhouse. Not long after, he shot the woman's boyfriend, a Cuban national, and dumped his body in a creek near San Antonio.

Resendiz also admitted to the murder of 33-year-old Michael White, battered to death with a brick in July 1991. He claims White made homosexual advances towards him.

Six years later, in 1997, Resendiz bludgeoned Jesse Howell, 19, to death with an air hose coupling, then raped and strangled his 16-year-old girlfriend Wendy Von Huben. The bodies were buried in a shallow grave in Sumter County, Florida. That same year, an unidentified transient was beaten to death with a piece of wood in a rail yard in Colton, California. Police consider Resendiz the prime suspect in that case.

Resendiz was, what is commonly referred to as, a disorganized killer. His crimes were not planned and he attacked victims of opportunity, his only requirement being that it was someone who couldn't fight back. He killed for whatever he needed, money, food, drugs, alcohol, a place to stay. He did rape some of his victims, but sex was a secondary motivation. Basically, in the words of former FBI profiler, John Douglas, he was "a bungling crook." But that worked in his favor. He, himself, didn't know where he was going next. He simply hopped the next freight train that came along. This made his travels haphazard and made him almost impossible to track down.

While his travels were spontaneous, and his killings best described as "rage-filled explosions," Resendiz was not without an identifying signature. All of his murders occurred close to train lines, and his M.O. was almost always the same. He'd scope out a home to see what he was up against, making sure there was no one who might get the upper hand on him. His preferred victims were women and the elderly. He'd break in, using his skills as a burglar. Once inside the residence, he'd find a weapon, usually a blunt-force trauma object. Then he'd launch his attack, bludgeoning the victim to death.

Afterward, he'd ransack the house before jumping the next freight out of town. Sometimes, he'd take the victim's car, on other occasions, he'd spend a couple of days living in the house before leaving.

Another characteristic of his signature was that he'd cover his victims' bodies with a blanket. Psychologists might suggest that he was ashamed and remorseful about what he'd done. But, with a brutal killer like Angel Resendiz, it's difficult to believe that the capacity for remorse existed at all.

The first murder of the spree that elevated him onto the FBI's Most Wanted List occurred on August 29, 1997, in Lexington, Kentucky. Christopher Maier, a 21-year-old University of Kentucky student was walking along the railroad tracks near the college with his girlfriend, Holly Dunn, when Reséndiz attacked them. Maier was bludgeoned to death with a rock, Dunn was beaten, raped, and left for dead. Miraculously, Holly Dunn survived.

Thirteen months later, on October 4, 1998, 87-year-old Leafie Mason was bludgeoned to death with a tire iron inside her home, just 50 yards from the railroad tracks in Hughes Spring, Texas.

Then, on December 17, 1998, Resendiz broke into the home of Dr. Claudia Benton, 39, in Houston, Texas. He waited until Dr. Benton returned home, then raped her before stabbing and beating her to death. Resendiz then left the scene in the victim's Jeep Cherokee, which was later found in San Antonio, Texas. Fingerprints lifted from the steering column were matched to Resendiz, and a warrant was issued for his arrest, although, bizarrely the charge was only burglary - not murder.

Yet despite the warrant, Resendiz struck again on May 2, 1999, in Weimar, Texas. Reverend Norman "Skip" Sirnic, 46, and wife Karen, 47, were bludgeoned to death with a sledgehammer in the parsonage of the United Church of Christ. The couple's red Mazda was found in San Antonio three weeks later, again with forensic evidence linking the murders to the Railroad Killer.

A month later, on June 2, the Border Patrol apprehended Resendiz near El Paso as he was trying to cross the border illegally. While he was in custody, the INS ran a computer check, to determine whether there were any outstanding arrest warrants on him. The search turned up nothing and he was deported to Mexico. Resendiz immediately found his way back to the States where, within 48 hours, he committed another two murders.

On June 4, 1999, Resendiz battered 26-year-old Noemi Dominguez to death in her Houston apartment. Seven days later, state troopers found Dominguez's white Honda Civic abandoned near the international bridge in Del Rio, Texas. And on the same day, the brutal killer bludgeoned 73-year-old Josephine Konvicka, using the same pick handle that had killed Noemi Dominguez. As with the other victims, Konvicka's home was located close to the railway lines.

By now, the elusive Railroad Killer had struck terror into the hearts of communities along the tracks from Texas to Illinois. In small towns where doors had traditionally stood unlocked at night, deadbolts were fixed. Shops closed early and children were ushered off the streets long before dark. Sporting goods stores saw a run on weapons and ammunition. Meanwhile, law enforcement agencies did what they could to find the wandering murderer. Freight yard security was stepped up and vagrants were hauled into local jails for questioning. Freight trains were stopped and searched. It did nothing to stop the killer.

On June 15, 1999, Resendiz broke into a mobile home in Gorham, Illinois where he shot 80-year-old George Morber, Sr. in the head with a shotgun, before clubbing Morber's daughter, Carolyn Frederick, to death. Mrs. Fredericks' red pickup truck was later spotted sixty miles away in Cairo, Illinois, driven by a man matching Resendiz's description.

In June 1999, the FBI placed the Railroad Killer on its Ten Most Wanted list, and a reward of $50,000 was posted for information leading to the capture of the fugitive. Within days the reward rose to $125,000 as various jurisdictions added their contributions.

In the meantime, arrest warrants were issued in Jackson County, Illinois, Louisville, Kentucky, and Fayette County, Texas, as DNA evidence linked Resendiz to the murders committed there.

Two hundred agents were now hunting Resendiz, and over 1,000 tips came in from members of the public. But still, he evaded them. In fact, Resendiz had already fled back to Mexico and was laying low.

Sometime in early June, a rookie Texas Ranger named Drew Carter approached Resendiz's sister, Manuela, to ask for her assistance in bringing him back to the States. At first, Manuela was resistant to the idea, but when Carter explained that Resendiz might eventually be killed by law officers and was also likely to kill again, she agreed to help.

To sweeten the deal, Carter offered three things: that Resendiz's safety would be guaranteed in prison; that he could receive regular visits from friends and family; and that Resendiz would undergo a psychiatric evaluation. He did not, as Resendiz would later claim, offer immunity from the death penalty (Carter would not have had the authority to offer such a deal).

On Monday, July 12, the Harris County D.A. put the offer in writing and it was passed via relatives to Angel Resendiz, who was hiding out in Ciudad Juarez. That same evening, he sent word that he would hand himself over the following day.

At 9 a.m. on Tuesday, July 13, Carter waited with Manuela and her pastor on a bridge connecting Zaragosa, Mexico, with El Paso. Then a truck pulled up and a diminutive man in dirty jeans got out. He walked across the bridge towards the waiting party, offering Carter a handshake as he approached. The elusive Railroad Killer was finally in custody.

Angel Resendiz went on trial for murder on May 8, 1999. On May 17, 1999, after 10 hours of deliberation, the jury returned a guilty verdict for first-degree, premeditated murder. Despite his lawyers' pleas, the Railroad Killer was sentenced to death.

He was executed by lethal injection in Huntsville, Texas, on June 27, 2006.

Dean Corll

The Candy Man

At around 8:25 on the morning of Wednesday, August 8, 1973, the dispatcher at the police department in Pasadena, Texas, received a frantic phone call. The caller identified himself as Elmer Wayne Henley and told the dispatcher that he'd killed a man. He gave his address as 2020 Lamar Drive and was told to wait there. A unit was immediately sent to the scene.

When the officers arrived, they saw three teenagers, two boys and a girl, standing in front of the house. One of the boys – a timid, skinny youth with a scraggly goatee beard, stepped forward. He said that he had made the call and confessed to being the shooter. The man he'd shot was named Dean Corll. Henley claimed he had fired in self-defense.

After taking a .22 pistol from Henley, the officer placed him and the other two teens (identified as Rhonda Williams and Tim Kerley) into the patrol car. He then entered the residence and found the body of a man, six-foot tall and muscular. He'd been shot six times, bullets lodging in his chest, shoulder, and head. The officer returned to the car and read Henley his Miranda rights. Then he summoned crime scene investigators and took the three teenagers in for questioning.

At this point, it looked like a drink and drug-induced homicide, an altercation between friends that had gone wrong. Detectives would soon learn that it was much more than that. They were about to be immersed in the biggest case of serial homicide in US history.

The first indicator should have been the house itself, in particular, the bedroom with its plastic sheeting covering the floors and a sinister plywood board equipped with handcuffs, ropes, and cords. Then there was the large hunting knife, the collection of dildos, the duct tape, rolls of plastic, glass tubes, and petroleum jelly. If that wasn't enough, they found a coffin-shaped plywood box, with air holes drilled in it and strands of human hair inside.

But the real revelation came back at police headquarters, where Wayne Henley soon made a stunning admission. He said that Dean Corll was a homosexual and a pedophile and that over the last three years, he (Henley) along with another youth named David Brooks, had procured dozens of teenage boys for Corll. Corll had then raped and tortured these boys before murdering them and disposing of their bodies at several burial sites.

The police were initially skeptical of Henley's claims, assuming that he was trying to justify his claim of self-defense in the shooting of Corll. But Henley was insistent, and when he started mentioning the names of some of Corll's victims, officers sat up and took notice. The names were familiar to them, all of the boys had been reported missing over the last few years. Furthermore, Henley said he could take the officers to four separate burial sites. If the numbers Henley was quoting were accurate, it would make Dean Corll the worst mass murderer in American history.

Dean Arnold Corll was born on December 24, 1939, in Fort Wayne, Indiana. His father, Arnold was strict with his son, while Dean's mother, Mary, tended to be overprotective. The marriage was not a happy one and, in 1946, the couple divorced. A reconciliation in 1950 ended in divorce again, three years later.

Dean went to stay with his mother, but his parents remained on amicable terms, and him, and his younger brother, Simon, remained in regular contact with their father. After the second divorce, Corll's mother married a traveling salesman by the name of Jake West and the family moved to the small town of Vidor, Texas. Not long after, Mary started a small candy company named 'Pecan Prince.' Dean and his brother were actively involved in the business, running the candy-making machines and packing the produce, which Jake West would sell on his sales route.

Corll's mother divorced Jake West in 1963 and started a new business, 'Corll Candy Company.' Dean was drafted into the US

Army that year and served 10 months before successfully applying for a hardship discharge, on the grounds that he was needed in the family business.

In 1965, the Corll Candy Company relocated to new premises, across the street from Helms Elementary School. It was here that Corll first acquired his infamous nickname, "The Candy Man," due to his habit of giving free candy to local children, particularly teenage boys. The company also employed a few local kids, and Corll was known to flirt with teenage male employees. He even installed a pool table in a back room, which became a hangout for local youths. It was here that he met 12-year-old David Brooks in 1967.

Brooks was initially just one of many boys who hung out in the room behind the store, but over time Corll became more and more attentive to him, giving him gifts of money and taking him on trips to various beaches. When Brooks's parents divorced, he went to live with his mother in Beaumont, 85 miles away. But when he visited his father in Houston, he often spent time at Corll's apartment. In 1970, when Brooks was 15, he and Corll became involved in a sexual relationship.

At around this time, Corll's mother moved to Colorado and, following the closure of the candy business, Corll found work as an electrician with the Houston Lighting and Power Company. He'd remain employed there until his death.

It is impossible to say what turned Dean Corll from a seemingly diligent, caring, young man to a sadistic torturer and murderer of teenage boys. He did seem to have an unhealthy interest in boys half his age and was most likely a pedophile. Still, as despicable as the acts of that particular breed of criminal are, few of them are mass murderers. And Dean Corll was about to embark on a deadly campaign.

The first known victim was an 18-year-old college freshman, named Jeffrey Konen, who disappeared while hitchhiking on September 25, 1970. He was last seen at the corner of Westheimer Road in the Uptown area of Houston, close to where Corll was living at the time. He'd be found, three years later, in a shallow grave at High Island Beach.

Brooks claimed that around this time he walked in on Corll assaulting two teenage boys. Corll promised Brooks a car in return for his silence and also made a standing offer of $200 for any youths Brooks was able to lure to Corll's apartment. Brooks accepted both proposals, receiving a green Chevrolet Corvette, and soon after, procuring two 14-year-olds for Corll.

The boys, James Glass and Danny Yates had been attending a religious rally in the Heights district of Houston when David Brooks approached them and asked if they wanted to hang out with him and drink some beer. Glass was a friend of Brooks who'd been to Corll's apartment before, so they readily agreed. Once there, Corll overpowered them, cuffed them to his torture board, and then raped and tortured them before strangling them to death.

He and Brooks later buried them beneath a boatshed that Corll had recently rented.

Six weeks after the murder of Glass and Yates, Brooks and Corll saw two teenage brothers named Donald and Jerry Waldrop walking towards a bowling alley. The boys were enticed into Corll's van, then driven to Corll's apartment, where they were raped, tortured, strangled, and subsequently buried in the boat shed.

Three more victims followed between March and May 1971. Fifteen-year-old Randell Harvey was abducted while cycling to his part-time job as a gas station attendant. He was killed by a single bullet to the head. David Hilligiest, 13, and Gregory Winkle, 16, were friends who were abducted and killed together on the afternoon of May 29, 1971. Soon after their disappearances, the parents of all three boys launched a frantic, but ultimately fruitless, search for their sons. All three would be found buried under Corll's boatshed in 1973.

On August 17, 1971, Corll and Brooks were out cruising when they spotted 17-year-old Ruben Watson Haney walking home from a movie. Like James Glass, Haney was a friend of David Brooks, and Brooks persuaded him to attend a party at Corll's new apartment on San Felipe Street. Haney accompanied the pair to Corll's home where he was strangled and then buried in the boat shed.

In September 1971, Corll moved again, this time to 915 Columbia Street. Two more youths were murdered at this address according to Brooks, although their identities remain unknown.

The next teenager that Brooks procured for Corll was Elmer Wayne Henley. However, for some unexplained reason, perhaps because he saw a kindred spirit, Corll decided not to kill Henley. Instead, he made Henley the same offer he'd made David Brooks - $200 for any boy he could lure to Corll's apartment.

According to Henley, he initially rejected Corll's offer. But, early in 1972, with his family in desperate need of money, he finally gave in. Corll was by now living at 925 Schuler Street, and Henley said that he and Corll picked up a youth and asked him if he wanted to join them in drinking beer and smoking pot. The boy agreed and once at the house, they restrained him using a ruse he and Corll had practiced beforehand. Henley cuffed his own hands behind his back, then freed himself using a key hidden in his back pocket. He then persuaded the youth to try it, but once his hands were cuffed, Henley walked out, leaving the boy alone with Corll.

The identity of this victim is not known, but it may have been Willard Branch, a 17-year-old who disappeared on February 9, 1972, and who was later found buried beneath the boatshed.

One month later, on March 24, 1972, Corll, working with both of his young accomplices, persuaded 18-year-old Frank Aguirre (an acquaintance of Henley) to drink beer and smoke marijuana with them. Aguirre agreed and followed the trio to Corll's home where Corll overpowered him and cuffed his hands behind his back.

Henley later claimed that he tried to persuade Corll not to kill Aguirre, but Corll refused. Nonetheless, Henley accepted his $200 payment and helped Corll and Brooks bury Aguirre at High Island Beach.

On April 20, 1972, Henley led another friend of his to his death at the hands of Dean Corll. Seventeen-year-old Mark Scott fought furiously for his life, but when Corll produced a gun he "just gave up" according to Henley. Scott was tied to the torture board and suffered the same fate as Frankie Aguirre. He was raped, tortured, and strangled, then buried at High Island Beach.

According to Brooks, Henley wasn't just a procurer for Corll, but an active and sadistic participant in the murders, especially those that occurred at Schuler Street. Before Corll moved from the address on June 26, Henley helped Corll and Brooks to abduct and murder two youths, Billy Baulch and Johnny Delone. In Brooks' later confession, he said that both boys were tied to Corll's bed and, after being tortured and raped, Henley manually strangled Baulch to death. He then shouted, "Hey, Johnny!" before shooting Delone in the head. The bullet exited through Delone's ear but didn't kill him. Then, as he pleaded for his life, Henley strangled him to death.

Another youth who was lured to Corll's Schuler Street residence was 19-year-old Billy Ridinger. Like the other victims, Ridinger was tied to the board, tortured and raped by Corll. However, Brooks claimed that he persuaded Corll to let Ridinger go. On another occasion, Brooks feared that he might, himself, become a victim. Henley knocked him unconscious as he entered the house, and he woke to find himself tied to Corll's bed. Corll raped him repeatedly but later released him. Despite the assault, Brooks continued to help Corll in the abduction of the victims.

Corll next moved to an apartment at Westcott Towers, where he is known to have killed two more victims. The first of these was 17-year-old Steven Sickman, last seen leaving a party just after midnight on July 20. He was savagely beaten with a blunt instrument before being strangled to death and buried in the boat shed. A month later, Roy Bunton, 19, was abducted while walking to work. He was shot twice in the head and was also buried in the boat shed.

Less than two months later, on October 2, 1972, Henley and Brooks persuaded two teenagers named Wally Jay Simoneaux and Richard Hembree to join them at Corll's apartment. That evening, Simoneaux's mother received a strange call from her son. He spoke only one word into the phone, a plaintive "Mama," before the connection was terminated. The next morning, Henley accidentally shot Hembree in the mouth and several hours later, both boys were strangled to death. They were buried in the boat shed, their bodies placed on top of those of James Glass and Danny Yates. The following month, a 19-year-old youth named Richard Kepner was abducted and murdered, and then buried at High Island Beach.

On January 20, 1973, Corll moved to Wirt Road in the Spring Branch district of Houston. Within two weeks of moving to this address, he killed a 17-year-old named Joseph Lyles, a friend of both Brooks and Corll. On March 7, Corll moved from Wirt Road to an address his father had recently vacated, 2020 Lamar Drive, Pasadena.

There were no further murders between February and June 3, 1973, although Corll is known to have been ill during this time and Henley was out of town, having moved to Mount Pleasant in an apparent effort to get away from Corll. When the killings did start up again, they started with a vengeance, and both Brooks and Henley would later testify that Corll had become more brutal than ever. His two accomplices had learned to recognize when Corll was getting ready to kill. He'd become reckless, smoking constantly and displaying twitchy reflex movements. Soon after, he'd announce that he "needed to do a new boy," and the unholy trio would hit the streets in search of victims.

On June 4, Henley and Corll abducted a 15-year-old named William Ray Lawrence. They raped and tortured the boy for three days before burying him at Lake Sam Rayburn. Less than two weeks later, 20-year-old Raymond Blackburn was abducted, strangled, and buried at the same location. Corll was accelerating now. On July 7, Homer Garcia, 15, an acquaintance of Henley's was shot, then left to bleed to death in Corll's bathtub and on July 12, a 17-year-old youth named John Sellars was shot to death and buried at High Island Beach.

In July 1973, David Brooks married his pregnant fiancée, and Henley temporarily became Corll's sole accomplice. Three more teenagers would die between July 19 and July 25; 15-year-old Michael Baulch was strangled and buried at Lake Sam Rayburn; Charles Cobble and Marty Ray Jones were abducted together and buried in the boat shed. These were the only abductions in which David Brooks did not play a part.

The last to die was also Corll's youngest victim. James Dreymala was just 13 years old when he was snatched from his bicycle on August 3, 1973. He was tied to Corll's torture board, raped, tortured, and strangled before being buried in the boat shed.

Four days later, Dean Corll would be dead, shot during an altercation with one of his accomplices.

On the evening of August 7, 1973, Henley brought a 19-year-old named Timothy Kerley to Corll's house in Pasadena, intending for him to be Corll's next victim. The two drank beer and sniffed paint until around midnight when they went to buy something to eat. While they were out, Kerley suggested picking up 15-year-old Rhonda Williams, a friend of both youths. Rhonda agreed to accompany them, but when they arrived, Corll was furious that Henley had brought a girl to his house. Eventually, Henley managed to calm Corll down and he offered the teenagers beer and marijuana. The three began drinking, sniffing paint fumes, and smoking pot, while Corll watched them intently. Eventually, they passed out.

Henley woke lying on his stomach with Corll snapping handcuffs onto his wrists. His mouth had been taped shut and his ankles bound together. Kerley and Williams lay beside Henley, securely bound and gagged, Kerley stripped naked.

Noticing that Henley was awake, Corll removed the gag from his mouth. He told Henley that he was going to kill all three of them after he'd raped and tortured Kerley. He then started kicking Rhonda Williams in the chest, then dragged Henley into the kitchen, and placed a gun to his stomach, threatening to shoot him. Henley managed to calm Corll down by promising to help torture and murder Williams and Kerley. Corll then uncuffed Henley, and the two of them carried Kerley and Williams to the bedroom and tied them to the torture board.

Corll instructed Henley to cut away Rhonda's clothes and rape her while he did likewise to Kerley. He began torturing and assaulting Kerley. Henley then asked Corll if he could take Rhonda into another room and when Corll ignored him, Henley suddenly grabbed Corll's gun.

"I can't go on any longer!" Henley shouted. "I can't have you kill all my friends!"

"Kill me, Wayne!" Corll said. Then, as he advanced towards Henley, "You won't do it!"

Henley fired one shot, hitting Corll in the forehead, then as Corll lurched forward, he fired twice more, striking Corll's left shoulder. Corll spun round and staggered towards the door before Henley fired three more shots into his lower back and shoulder. Henley then released Kerley and Williams and after some discussion, they called the police.

The monster was dead, but police still had to find closure for the families of the victims.

Wayne Henley led police to Corll's boatshed, where he claimed most of the victims were buried. As they began digging they soon uncovered the body of a young blond-haired boy, lying on his side, wrapped in clear plastic and buried beneath a layer of lime. As the evacuations continued more remains were found, in varying stages of decomposition. Some victims had been shot, others strangled, the ligatures still wrapped tightly around their necks.

All of the victims had been sodomized and most bore clear evidence of sexual torture: pubic hairs plucked out, genitals chewed, objects inserted into their rectums, glass rods shoved into their penises and smashed. In many cases, rags had been inserted into the victims' mouths and secured with adhesive tape to muffle their screams. In some instances, Corll had castrated his live victims: severed genitals were found inside several sealed plastic bags.

On August 8, 1973, a total of eight corpses were uncovered at the boatshed. That same day David Brooks handed himself over to the Houston Police. He denied participating in any of the murders, saying only that he knew of two murders Corll had committed in 1970.

The following day, August 9, Henley gave a written statement detailing his and Brooks' involvement and there were nine more bodies recovered from the boat shed. Henley also accompanied police officers to Lake Sam Rayburn in San Augustine County, where two more bodies were found in shallow graves.

Faced with the mounting evidence against him, David Brooks gave a full confession that evening, admitting to being present at several of the murders and helping with several of the burials. He continued to deny direct participation in the killings.

On August 10, two more bodies were found buried at Lake Sam Rayburn and police began their search at High Island Beach, where two more victims were found, interred in shallow graves. Three days later, Henley and Brooks again accompanied the police to High Island Beach, where four more bodies were found, taking the total of twenty-seven known victims – at the time the worst killing spree in American history.

Elmer Wayne Henley and David Owen Brooks were tried separately for their roles in the murders. Henley was brought to trial in San Antonio on July 1, 1974, charged with six murders. He was found guilty and sentenced to six consecutive 99-year terms - a total of 594 years – meaning he will never see the outside of a prison cell.

David Brooks stood trial on February 27, 1975, accused of four murders committed between December 1970 and June 1973. He was found guilty on one charge and sentenced to life imprisonment without the possibility of parole.

Nannie Doss

The Giggling Granny

Nancy Hazle, later to achieve infamy as Nannie Doss, was born on November 4, 1905, in Blue Mountain, Alabama. Her parents were poor farmers, her father, James, a man of volatile temper who was often violent to his wife Lou, and his children, three girls and a boy besides Nancy.

Life was tough for young Nannie (as she was called from childhood). By the age of five, she was required to cut wood, plow the fields, and clear the land of weeds and rocks. Evenings were spent at chores and the children were required to be up before daybreak. They attended school intermittently. If James Hazle decided he needed help with the backbreaking work around the farm, his children were held back from their schooling to aid in the task. Friends and games were strictly forbidden, leisure time a distant dream.

One rare break from the daily drudgery occurred in 1912 when Nannie was seven years old. However, this event produced an incident that she'd later blame for her murderous nature. She'd gone with her family to visit a relative in downstate Alabama, the train ride providing a rare thrill for the unsophisticated young girl. On the journey, the train was forced to make an emergency stop, pitching Nannie out of her chair to slam her head into the metal frame of the seat in front of her. She'd later claim that after this incident she suffered from pains and blackouts for months, and for the rest of her life was afflicted by headaches and mood swings.

As Nannie, grew older she began to take an interest in her mother's romance magazines, in particular, the ads for Lonely Hearts clubs. She dreamed of being swept off her feet by her own Prince Charming, but there was little opportunity for meeting boys. Her father saw to that. He strictly forbade his daughters from attending the church socials and Saturday night dances. Make-up was out of the question and he told them that only whores wore silk stockings and tight dresses. Any kind of modern hairstyle was also strictly taboo. James Hazle saw his daughters primarily as farm labor and he wasn't about to give them up easily. Besides, when they got to marriageable age, he intended to pick out their husbands himself.

Despite Pa Hazle's strict curfews, Nannie did, on occasion, manage to sneak away for an assignation. Boys liked her. She was reasonably pretty with dark hair and dark eyes and quite easy to talk into a hayloft. In modern parlance, Nannie Hazle was easy.

In 1921, Nannie found work at the Linen Thread Company, where a co-worker, Charley Braggs, took a fancy to her. Her father approved. Young Charley was a serious young man who doted on his elderly mother. Later that year, the 16-year-old Nannie walked down the aisle and became Mrs. Braggs.

Charlie was tall and handsome, but if Nannie thought she'd found her Prince she was soon disavowed of that notion. Her new husband was a mommy's boy whose mother controlled his life. Soon she was controlling Nannie's life, too.

During the first four years of their marriage, Nannie bore Charley four daughters, the first, Melvina, in 1923, and the last, Florine, in 1927. As the pressures of living with a demanding mother-in-law, raising four young children, and keeping house for a weak-willed husband got to her, she sought solace in booze and became a chain smoker. Soon she was also hanging out at various taverns and conducting casual affairs with other men. Not that Charley Bragg cared, by this time he was a drunk himself and had other mistresses around town.

Then, in 1927, a tragedy befell the Bragg family – they lost their two middle daughters to suspected food poisoning.

Although the deaths were ruled accidental, one person wasn't convinced. Charley Bragg had long suspected that his wife was trying to kill him, and had for years refused to eat or drink anything that Nannie prepared while in "one of her moods." Now he took his oldest daughter, Melvina, and fled the jurisdiction.

When he eventually returned, a year later, it was with another woman. Nannie could take a hint. She packed her belongings, and departed with her two daughters, leaving Charlie alone with his new woman. Charley Braggs was lucky. Nannie's next four husbands wouldn't enjoy the same good fortune.

Nannie returned to her parent's home and found a job at a cotton mill in nearby Anniston. Although the hours were long and the work hard, there were compensations. Nanny was still a good-looking woman, and she appreciated the admiring glances she attracted from the men in the shop. Still, she wasn't going to make the same mistake again. When she gave her heart, it would be to a man of sophistication, not some country bumpkin.

She took to scanning the Lonely hearts column in the local newspaper and soon took an interest in a 23-year-old factory worker named Frank Harrelson. Frank wrote well and his picture showed him to be a handsome young man who reminded her of her matinee idol, Clark Gable. He lived in nearby Jacksonville, and it wasn't long before he arrived on Nannie's doorstep. Instantly smitten, he proposed soon after and Nannie accepted. They were married in 1929.

For a few months, the couple was blissfully happy, but it soon became clear to

Nannie that her new husband had a problem with booze. A serious problem, in fact, Frank was an alcoholic. Not only that, but she discovered that he had done jail time for felonious assault, something he'd neglected to share with her. Neither had prison done anything to dull his violent ways. At least once a week, the police would knock on her door to inform her that Frank had been arrested for drunken brawling. And his violence wasn't confined to his drinking buddies, sometimes he'd use his fists on Nannie, sometimes on her daughters.

By the early 1940s, those daughters, Melvina and Florine, were grown and married. Melvina had a son, Robert, in 1943, and, in 1944 fell pregnant again. The birth, in February 1945, was difficult. Like a good mother, Nannie remained with her daughter throughout the night, nursing and encouraging her. Eventually, just after dawn, Melvina gave birth to a healthy baby girl. Soon after, she fell into a fevered sleep. Her husband, Mosie, who'd been awake through the night, dozed off in the chair next to her.

At one point, Melvina woke from her stupor and looked across to where her mother stood, cradling the newborn. She was only awake for a short while, and would later be uncertain whether what she witnessed was real or a nightmare, but she thought she saw Nannie push a hatpin into the baby's tender head.

Weak and groggy from painkilling drugs, she dozed off again. When she awoke, a doctor told her that her baby was dead. The doctor could not explain the death, but Melvina was bothered by what she thought she'd seen. A few days later, she spoke to her sister, Florine, about it. Florine was startled. She said that she'd seen their mother turning a hatpin over in her fingers earlier that evening.

Within six months there was another tragedy. After a falling out with her husband, Melvina had gone to stay with relatives for a short while, leaving her infant son, Robert, in Nannie's care. A few days later the little boy was dead. Doctors diagnosed his death as "asphyxia" and Nannie was devastated. However, several months later, she collected the payout on a $500 insurance policy she'd taken out on the boy's life.

Nannie pocketed her windfall and began plotting how to get rid of the next impediment in her life. Frank Harrelson had continued to drink and to use Nannie as a punching bag when the need took him. On the night of September 15, 1945, Frank was out at a tavern, celebrating with friends who'd just returned from fighting the war in Europe. He arrived home still in a festive mood and demanded sex from his wife. When she refused, he slammed her up against a wall and threatened her.

Nannie relented but decided then and there that she would have her revenge. Her opportunity came the next day. While tending her garden, she found a corn liquor jar that her husband had hidden in the flower bed. Picking up the jar, she carried it to the storeroom, poured away some of the liquid, and topped it with rat poison. Later that evening, Frank Harrelson died in excruciating pain.

After Frank's death, Nannie took to traveling the country, usually by rail. Where she went, and what she got up to, is anyone's guess, but we do know that, in 1947, she detrained in the scenic little town of Lexington, North Carolina. Nannie was there to visit Arlie Lanning, a man she'd met through a lonely-hearts ad. Two days after their initial meeting, the couple was married.

Life with Arlie wasn't the constant drama that it had been with Frank Harrelson, but it was no bed of roses either. Like his predecessor, Arnie was a boozer and a womanizer, but Nannie had a novel way of dealing with his indiscretions. Whenever things got too much for her, she simply took off, sometimes staying away for months on end. No one knew where she went, but she'd sometimes send Arlie a telegram. These came from all over the country. Nannie, it seemed, traveled without plan or purpose, going wherever the mood took her.

Then suddenly she'd be back and Arlie would promise to go on the wagon and stop chasing women, promises he'd break soon thereafter. On the home front, Nannie played the perfect wife, cooking, cleaning, and caring for her man. She still got her kicks reading romance magazines, but she had a new obsession now – television. When there was a love story on the tube, Arlie didn't dare bother her. She'd sit with her feet up and slowly work her way through a pack of Camels, while the grayscale drama played out.

During her time in Lexington, Nannie was also an avid churchgoer and a well-liked member of the congregation. Many in the flock couldn't understand how a respectable woman like Nannie could stay married to a rapscallion like Arnie, whose exploits in the town's less salubrious taverns were a common topic of scandal.

So when Arnie died in February 1950, most of those at the funeral were there to support the bereaved widow, rather than to mourn the deceased. Arlie had died suddenly, but no one was surprised, the man was a notorious drunk after all. And if his symptoms - sweating, vomiting, dizziness - didn't exactly tie in with the given cause of death, heart failure, nobody bothered to check.

On April 21, eight weeks after Arlie's death, the home he and Nannie had shared burned to the ground, a stroke of luck for Nannie because it had been bequeathed, in Arlie's will, to his sister. The insurance company issued a check to "Arlie Lanning, deceased," and it was duly cashed by his widow. Nannie, who had been living with Arlie's mother, left town soon after, but not before the elderly Mrs. Lanning died mysteriously in her sleep.

Nannie's next move was to Gadsden, Alabama, where she stayed for a while with her cancer-stricken sister, Dovie. Nannie insisted on taking full responsibility for her sibling's care, and Dovie's condition soon after began to go steadily downhill. She died on June 30, 1950.

By 1952, Nannie was no longer the attractive young woman she'd once been, she'd put on weight, acquired a double chin, and now wore thick glasses. Still, her quest for romance was undiminished and she soon met a new suitor through the "Diamond Circle Club," a monthly newsletter for those seeking love and marriage.

His name was Richard L. Morton. He was from Emporia, Kansas and he described himself as a retired businessman. Nannie was now 47, but she still had her feminine wiles about her, and Morton was soon besotted. They wed in October 1952.

At first, Morton seemed like the man of her dreams, tall, dark, and handsome. He was also ever so attentive, showering Nannie with gifts of clothes and jewelry. But it soon became clear that, despite his extravagance, Morton was flat broke and deep in hock to everyone. He also had another woman, and he had no intention of giving her up.

Nannie seems to have decided early in the marriage that Morton wouldn't do. By Christmas, just two months after they were wed, she was already back to her old routine of writing letters in reply to Lonely Hearts ads.

But Nannie's murderous plans for husband number four were delayed by the death of Pa Hazle. After the funeral, Nannie's mother announced that she was coming to stay, a bad move on her part. She'd been in her daughter's home only a few days when she suddenly took ill with chronic stomach pains. Not long after, she joined her husband in the ground.

Three months later, Nannie had another funeral to attend when her husband Richard Morton died, his symptoms remarkably similar to those of Lou Hazle's. And still no one – not friends or family, doctors or even the police - asked any questions.

Nannie's fifth husband was markedly different from the others. Sam Doss was a serious, God-fearing man. He didn't drink or smoke or chase women, wasn't interested in gambling, and was never heard to swear. He was impeccably turned out at all times, extremely thrifty, and seldom became excited about any cause. In other words, he was boring.

Nanny might have tolerated that (she'd had her fill of hard-drinking, hard-living men, after all) but what she wouldn't tolerate was his insistence that radio, television, and her beloved romance magazines had no place in a Christian household. She also soon tired of his rigidly enforced schedule, and his tight fist on the purse strings. Eventually, she'd had enough and hopped a bus to Alabama.

It was a ruse, but it worked. Doss came after her like a jilted teenager, pleading for forgiveness and promising to change his ways. To show his contriteness, he lavished his wife with gifts and gave her signing powers on his bank account. And then he made a deadly mistake. He took out an insurance policy on his life, naming Nannie as his beneficiary.

Not long after, Doss awoke one night with severe stomach pains. Such was his affliction that he was unable to stand and was bedridden for days, with Nannie tending him. His condition showed no improvement. In fact, it got worse, and his doctor admitted him to hospital. There, over 23 days, he gradually improved enough to go home.

He was discharged from the hospital on October 5 and, to celebrate his return, Nannie cooked a roast pork dinner, which Doss consumed heartily, finishing with a cup of coffee that his wife had prepared. By morning, Sam Doss was dead.

But Nannie had made a mistake this time. In her rush to rid herself of husband number five and, perhaps frustrated by the delay caused by his hospitalization, she'd given Doss a massive dose of arsenic. The doctor who'd discharged him from the hospital called for an autopsy. It showed up enough poison to kill a dozen men.

Nannie Doss was promptly arrested, but despite hours of intense interrogation she continued to deny complicity in Sam's death. Eventually, though, she confessed to killing Doss by spiking his coffee with arsenic. Then with that out of the way, she confessed that she'd killed Richard Morton, Arlie Lanning, and Frank Harrelson, too.

The morning after her confession, exhumations of her husbands, her mother, her sister Dovie, her nephew Robert, and her mother-in-law, Mrs. Lanning, were ordered. Arsenic was found in all of the deceased spouses and in her mother. The other bodies, which showed no trace of toxins, appeared to have died by asphyxiation, perhaps by being smothered in their sleep.

Nannie Doss' trial was set for June 2, 1955, but she circumvented events by pleading guilty on May 17. She was sentenced to life in the Oklahoma State Penitentiary and died there, of leukemia, in 1965.

Gary Ray Bowles

The Gay Slayer

On Saturday, November 19, 1994, Belinda Hinton arrived at her brother Jay's mobile home in Duval County, Florida. Belinda was concerned. The previous day, she'd celebrated her birthday, and Jay had promised to be there but hadn't shown. It was unlike Jay to let her down, the two of them were close.

Although the lights in the home were on, a sharp rap at the door produced no response and as Jay's Cadillac was nowhere to be seen, Belinda assumed that he had gone out. A little annoyed, she left, only to return later.

Over the next two days, Belinda returned several times, in the company of her fiancé, William. Eventually, concerned that Jay may have suffered an accident, they decided to break in. William managed to shatter a pane and open the back door. But the minute they stepped inside, they knew that something was terribly wrong. A foul smell pervaded the building and there were signs that a struggle had occurred.

A search of the bedroom turned up nothing, but in the bathroom, William saw a mound of blankets on the floor. Underneath lay the battered and decomposing corpse of Jay Hinton. William quickly hustled his fiancée outside, then ran to the neighbors and called the police.

Investigators arriving at the home found a chaotic scene – blood spattered on the bathroom floor and walls, beer cans and alcohol miniatures strewn throughout, the victim's personal papers scattered across the bedroom. They also found the likely murder weapon, a large, blood-drenched, stepping-stone, weighing approximately 40 pounds and more than likely carried in from the front yard. Lastly, detectives discovered a receipt made out to "Timothy Whitfield." They saw too, that the victim's car was missing.

The body was removed to the morgue, where the medical examiner noted severe trauma to the head and face. Jay's forehead and cheekbone had been smashed, consistent with being struck by a heavy object. In addition, he had five broken ribs, plus various abrasions to his arms and legs. Severe though these injuries were they were not the cause of death. Jay Hinton had been strangled, the process of asphyxiation aided by toilet paper and rags being forced down his throat. He'd been dead for at least three days.

It didn't take investigators long to turn up a suspect in the murder. Several witnesses reported that a man named Timothy Whitfield had been living with Jay as a houseguest. A composite sketch was drawn up and circulated. Two days later, it paid dividends.

On October 22, 1994, the police tracked Whitfield to a labor pool at Jacksonville Beach. Taken into custody, the 32-year-old admitted his true identity. He was Gary Ray Bowles, a name police were well aware of. In fact, Bowles was currently on the FBI's Ten Most

Wanted List, a suspect in a series of brutal slayings ranging from Maryland to Florida.

Gary Ray Bowles was born on January 25, 1962, in Clifton Forge, Virginia. His father, William Franklin Bowles, died before Gary was born, and his mother, Frances Carole Price Bowles, remarried several times.

According to Frances' later court testimony, Gary had a good early childhood. However, from the age of seven, he began to suffer violent abuse by his first stepfather. His mother confessed that her husband often beat Gary and his older brother, using a belt or his fists. When she tried to intervene, she too was beaten. Eventually, she divorced her husband and later remarried a man named Chet.

Francis seems to have been a singularly bad judge of character. Chet was even more violent than his predecessor. Any time he drank (which was often), he'd fly into a rage and beat Francis and her sons. Several times, he put her in the hospital. Faced with abuse and battery at home, Gary sought solace in glue sniffing and delinquency. As a ten-year-old, he was already using harder drugs and alcohol and regularly skipping school. He'd drop out completely in the eighth grade.

Meanwhile, his stepfather continued using him as a punching bag until, when Gary was 13, and his brother was 14, they ganged up on the man and delivered a savage beating of their own. Thereafter, they demanded that their mother dump Chet. When she refused, Gary left home for good.

Just 13, and living on the streets, Gary supported himself by prostitution. He wasn't gay, though, and would later state that he only allowed men to perform oral sex on him. He never performed fellatio himself, nor engaged in intercourse. It was purely a financial endeavor, driven by the need to survive.

During this time, he had several relationships with women, but as is so often the case with victims of abuse, he became abusive himself. One particularly violent relationship occurred during the early 80s when he lived in Hillsborough County, Florida, with a woman named Wesley. In June 1982, he beat the woman so severely that there were blood spatters against the wall, reaching five feet above the bed. Wesley was also subjected to a brutal rape that left her with severe lacerations to her vagina and rectum. That attack earned Gary Bowles a six-year jail term.

Not long after his release, Bowles was in trouble again. In July 1991, he attacked a woman and snatched her purse before fleeing.

Apprehended soon after, he was sent down for another four-year term. Not long after his release he embarked on the killing spree that would elevate him onto the FBI's "Ten Most Wanted Fugitives List."

Bowles' killing spree started on April 14, 1994. On that date, Daytona police were called to the residence of 59-year-old John Hardy Roberts.

It was clear that a violent struggle had taken place, blood spattered everywhere, furniture overturned, a coffee table and glass lamp shattered. Roberts' badly beaten body lay on the living room floor. He'd been strangled, and a rag had been stuffed down his throat. His head also showed signs of severe trauma and one of his fingers was almost severed from his hand.

There was little doubt as to the perpetrator. Gary Ray Bowles was known to have been living as a houseguest of the deceased. His fingerprints and probation papers were found at the scene and he'd made numerous phone calls to his family from Roberts' home. Moreover, the victim's car and wallet were missing and police soon learned that Bowles had tried to use the dead man's credit cards.

A manhunt was launched with investigators eventually tracking Roberts' car to Georgia. Bowles, though, had already fled to Maryland, where investigators were called to the scene of another murder.

On April 14, 1994, a maintenance man found the decomposing corpse of 38-year-old David Jarman in the basement of his Silver Spring home. Like Roberts, Jarman had been savagely beaten and strangled, a rag shoved down his throat. The victim's car and wallet were also missing. Witness reports suggested that Jarman had been seen at a gay bar in Washington, D.C., accompanied by a man matching Bowles' description.

Bowles meanwhile had moved on to Savannah, Georgia, where, on May 5, the body of 72-year-old Milton Bradley was discovered hidden behind a shed at a golf club. Bradley had been brutally beaten before being strangled. Like Bowles' other victims, he had rags pushed down his throat, which had aided asphyxiation.

Bradley had been a well-known and well-loved citizen of Savannah, a World War II veteran, a quiet and gentle man known for his generosity and kindness. He suffered from a slight mental impairment, which had no doubt made him easy prey for a predator like Bowles.

And although Milton Bradley did not match the profile of his other victims, there was no doubt that Bowles was responsible. Several witnesses had seen Bradley in the presence of a man matching

Bowles's description. More tellingly, a palm print lifted from the scene was positively matched to Bowles.

In July, the television program America's Most Wanted filmed a segment about the crimes Bowles was suspected of. After it was aired, police received numerous tips from viewers, although none of them got investigators any closer to the elusive fugitive.

Then, on May 19, the body of 37-year-old Albert Morris was found in his trailer in Nassau County, Florida. He'd been battered with a blunt object, shot in the chest, and strangled. Morris also had a towel stuffed into his mouth and his car and wallet were missing.

The murder bore all of the hallmarks of Gary Ray Bowles, and eyewitness reports placed him at the scene. Bowles had met Morris at a Jacksonville gay bar and spent two weeks living in Morris' trailer. On the night of the murder, the two men had been ejected from a bar after getting into a raucous argument.

Not long after, the FBI, who had long been involved in the investigation, discovered another murder that fit Bowles' signature. Alverson Carter Jr. was found beaten and strangled to death in his Atlanta home. A cloth had also been rammed down his throat and forensic evidence found at the scene confirmed Bowles as the perpetrator.

Bowles dropped from sight after the Carter homicide and is not believed to have committed any murders between May and November when Jay Hinton made the grave mistake of offering him a place to stay.

Now in custody, Bowles provided investigators with a detailed description of the Hinton murder. It is instructive in understanding Bowles's rage-filled M.O.

Bowles said that he met Hinton in early November 1994, at Jacksonville Beach. After spending several days together, Hinton moved to a trailer in Duval County and invited Bowles to stay with him for a while.

Bowles stayed for about two weeks. During that time, there was an altercation after Hinton accused Bowles of behaving inappropriately towards a female friend of his. Hinton asked Bowles to leave, however, they patched up their differences and he was allowed to stay.

On the day of the murder, Bowles had been partying with a friend of Hinton's named Rick. When Hinton returned from work, they continued drinking beer and smoking pot until 8 p.m., when Rick had to leave.

Hinton drove Rick to the train station with Bowles in the backseat. They continued drinking and smoking pot as they waited for the train to arrive. Rick would later testify that, by the time he left, Bowles was intoxicated, but still in control of his faculties.

After Rick caught his train, Hinton and Bowles returned to the trailer where Bowles continued drinking, while Hinton retired to bed. There were still tensions between the two men due to their previous argument when Hinton had asked Bowles to leave. Bowles said that, while he sat there simmering, something inside him snapped.

He went outside, picked up one of the stepping-stones, brought it into the house, and put it on the counter. He sat for a while staring at the stone and then picked it up and carried it to the bedroom. As Hinton lay sleeping, Bowles lifted the heavy rock and dropped it on his head. Stunned by the blow, Hinton woke and tried to flee, Bowles then followed him into the bathroom where he battered him into submission before shoving rags and toilet paper down his throat and then strangling him.

Afterward, he took Hinton's car and fled the scene, but returned soon after and stayed two more days with the corpse wrapped in blankets in the bathroom. He even brought a female acquaintance back to the trailer and she was unaware of the dead body, just feet away.

On December 8, 1994, Gary Bowles was indicted for the first-degree murder of Jay Hinton. He entered a guilty plea, meaning the sole function of the jury was to determine his punishment. They duly obliged, recommending the death penalty by a vote of ten to two. Judge Jack M. Schemer then made the sentence official.

Gary Ray Bowles is currently imprisoned at the Union Correctional Institute in Raiford, Florida, where he is expected to remain until his date with the executioner.

Edmund Kemper

The Co-ed Killer

"This craving, this awful raging eating feeling inside, this fantastic passion. It was overwhelming me. It was like drugs. It was like alcohol. A little wasn't enough." - Ed Kemper

The beautiful beach community of Santa Cruz lies south of San Francisco on the Pacific Coast. It is a haven for tourists, surrounded as it is, by majestic mountains, rugged coastline, and towering redwood trees. But in the early 1970s, Santa Cruz acquired a rather less desirable reputation. It became known as "Murder City," or alternately, "The Murder Capital of the World."

And with good reason too, during this time a trio of deadly psychopaths stalked the small town. First, there was John Linley Frazier, a crazed hippy who murdered five people in a bloody spree in 1970. Then there was Herb Mullin, a deeply psychotic young man who murdered 13 people in the belief that it would prevent an earthquake. And finally, there was Edmund Emil

Kemper III – 6 foot 9 inches, 300 pounds, of murderous fury, a killer and mutilator of 10, including his mother and grandparents.

Edmund Kemper was born in Burbank, California on December 18, 1948, the middle child, and only son, of Edmund Kemper Jr. and his wife, Clarnell. Ed was close to his father and devastated when his parents divorced in 1957. Shortly thereafter, Clarnell moved the family to Montana, and it was there that Edmund's problems first began to manifest.

By the time he was ten, Ed was already developing violent fantasies about murdering his mother, fantasies which soon branched out to include all women. He began to play bizarre games where he pretended to be executed in the gas chamber. He would cut the heads off his sisters' dolls. On one occasion his sister teased him about having a crush on his teacher. She asked Ed why he didn't kiss her, to which the 10-year-old replied, "If I did that, I'd have to kill her first."

These were worrying signs in a child so young, and his mother didn't help. She constantly berated and harangued Edmund, even locking him in the cellar because she believed he might harm his sisters. When he was 13, Kemper killed and decapitated the family cat, placing its head on a stick. At around the same time he ran away from home. He wanted to live with his father, but by now Kemper Sr. was remarried, with a new family. He allowed Ed to stay for a day or two, before sending him back to his mother. Her solution was to pack Edmund off to his paternal grandparent's ranch in North Fork, California.

Edmund hated it in North Fork. He found his grandmother as argumentative and as dominant as his mother and the two quarreled frequently. Matters eventually came to a head on August 27, 1964, eight months after Kemper had moved in. On that August afternoon, the 15-year-old boy (already an awkward, gangly, six-foot-four), got into yet another argument with his grandmother, Maude. Enraged, Kemper fetched the .22 rifle he'd been given as a Christmas present and shot the 66-year-old woman in the head. Then he waited for his grandfather to return from the grocery store and shot him too. Later he'd say that he'd killed his grandmother to "see how it feels," and his grandfather to "spare him the anguish of finding his wife dead."

Not knowing what else to do, Kemper then called his mother in Montana and told her what he had done. She instructed him to call the police, which he did, waiting calmly at the ranch until they arrived.

Kemper was placed with the California Youth Authority. Then he was sent for psychiatric evaluation, diagnosed as a paranoid schizophrenic, and transferred to the Atascadero State Hospital for the Criminally Insane, where he would remain until his release on his 21st birthday. Psychiatrists strongly recommended that Kemper should not live with his mother, but given that he had no place else to go, he moved back in with Clarnell in 1969.

☐

Kemper's mother had just divorced her third husband and taken a job as an administrative assistant at the new university in Santa

Cruz. She'd recently moved into a duplex on Ord Drive in Aptos when Ed came to stay with her. Before long, they were back into their old routine, getting into fierce arguments that the neighbors could hear through the walls. Kemper would later say that his mother was constantly on his case, bickering and sniping and criticizing everything he did, attacking his manhood and his sense of worth.

As part of his parole requirements, Kemper attended a community college and did well. He hoped to be accepted into the police force but was turned down because he was too tall. Disappointed, he began hanging out at "The Jury Room," a bar frequented by police officers. There, he became well-known to many of the cops. He was polite and soft-spoken, his speech intelligent and articulate. The cops liked him, and gave him the nickname, "Big Ed."

Kemper worked at several short-term jobs during this time, before landing a position with the California Highway Department. Soon he'd saved enough money to move out of his mother's home. He relocated to Alameda, near San Francisco, sharing an apartment with a friend. He bought a motorcycle, but his childhood clumsiness hadn't left him and he was involved in two accidents, one of which earned him a $15,000 insurance payout.

With this unexpected windfall, Kemper bought a yellow Ford Galaxy and began to cruise the highways. He also started picking up female hitchhikers, learning how to sweet-talk them into his car, how to allay any fears they might have about his huge bulk. By his estimation, he picked up as many as 150 female hikers without harming any of them. But, gradually, he began to prepare his vehicle for what he had in mind, stocking it with plastic bags, knives, a blanket, and handcuffs. The need was growing. Finally, when his drive to kill became too much, he acted.

According to Kemper's later confession, his first attempts at killing hitchhikers met with failure. He said he'd pick up a girl and drive her to a remote spot, only to realize that he couldn't go through with it. That changed on May 7, 1972. On that day, Kemper picked up two 18-year-old college students named Mary Anne Pesce and Anita Luchessa. The girls were hiking to Stanford, about an hour away, and were grateful for the ride. But that gratitude soon turned to terror as Kemper pulled off the highway and stopped on a dirt road. Using a gun to keep the women quiet, he told them he was going to rape them, then handcuffed Pesce in the back seat, and forced Luchessa into the trunk. He then placed a bag over Pesce's head and tried to strangle her, but she struggled so much that he drew his knife and began stabbing her, delivering blow after blow as the terrified woman screamed in pain and terror. Eventually, Kemper cut her throat, then went to the trunk, dragged out Anita Luchessa, and killed her too.

Carrying out the murders had not gone as smoothly as he had imagined in his fantasies, but he now had what he wanted, two corpses under his control, all his. Kemper moved the bodies into the trunk and drove back to his apartment. On the way home he was pulled over by a highway patrolman for a broken taillight, but he remained calm and cooperative and got off with a warning. He said later that if the officer had asked him to open the trunk, he'd have killed him on the spot.

Kemper's roommate was out when he got to the apartment, so he wrapped the bodies in blankets and carried them upstairs. Once inside, he laid the dead girls out on the floor of his bedroom, where he photographed them. Then he began dismembering the corpses, stopping to take photographs and to perform sexual acts on them. Later, he packed the body parts into bags and buried them in a shallow grave in the mountains. His final outrage was to use Mary Anne Pesce's severed head for fellatio, before discarding it in a ravine.

After the double murder, Kemper went back to picking up female hikers and delivering them safely to their destinations. He would even warn his passengers against accepting rides from strangers. But the need was growing again. On September 14, 1972, he gave in to it.

Aiko Koo was a fifteen-year-old schoolgirl who had just missed the bus and was late for a dance class. She was grateful when Kemper picked her up but soon regretted accepting the ride as he drove right past the dance studio and kept going. Eventually, he stopped on a remote road where he produced a gun and told the terrified girl that he was going to rape her. Koo immediately started screaming and Kemper, perhaps confused by this turn of events, scrambled out of the car and slammed the door accidentally locking himself out.

Koo was now locked inside the vehicle with the keys and Kemper's gun. Had she been thinking clearly, she might have used the weapon to protect herself or perhaps even driven off and left Kemper stranded. Instead, she allowed Kemper to sweet-talk her into opening the door. He responded by immediately grabbing her by the throat and strangling her to death. Thereafter, he raped her corpse before stuffing it in the trunk and driving off. On the way home, he even made a stop at his favorite bar to talk with his cop buddies. Then he drove to his apartment where he photographed and decapitated Koo and had sex with her headless corpse.

The day after he killed Aiko Koo, Ed Kemper went before a panel of psychiatrists, as required by the conditions of his parole. The panel noted that he'd done well in school, that he had a steady job, and that he'd stayed out of trouble. Kemper, by now well versed in the whole psychiatric evaluation routine, told them exactly what they wanted to hear. Suitably impressed, they declared Ed "normal," "safe," and, "no danger to anyone." Yet even as the psychiatrists signed the order sealing his juvenile record, Kemper was keeping a deadly secret. In the trunk of his car, parked downstairs in the lot, lay the severed head of Aiko Koo.

Having been given a clean bill of mental health, Kemper drove away and buried Koo's remains near Boulder Creek. Then he lay low for a while, fueling his fantasies with the sickening photographs he'd taken of his three victims. But the pressure soon began to build, and before long he began hunting for another victim.

On January 7, 1973, Kemper offered a ride to a pretty, 19-year-old student, named Cindy Schall. He drove her to a secluded spot where he produced a .22 pistol and shot her in the head. By now, Kemper was again living with his mother, so he drove back to her house, where he dismembered Schall's body in the bathtub. He kept the remains in his room overnight, before burying the head in the backyard and later throwing the body parts over a cliff. They quickly washed up on a beach, but no one suspected Kemper. He was free to kill again.

On February 5, after yet another argument with his mother, Kemper picked up Rosalind Thorpe. Then, with Thorpe in the passenger seat, he picked up another student, Allison Liu. Following his now-established M.O., Kemper waited until they were in a remote area, then pulled over, ostensibly to admire the view. As Thorpe turned to look, Kemper removed a pistol from the side panel and shot her in the head, killing her instantly. He then turned and fired four shots at Liu, sitting in the back seat, hitting her in the hand and the temple.

Like most serial killers, Kemper had refined his methodology with each successive kill. He quickly dragged the bodies to the trunk and mopped up any blood in the car. Then he drove back to his mother's house, where he spent the night in an orgy of necrophilia and dismemberment, capturing every sickening act on camera. The following morning, he scattered the remains, dropping some in the ocean, others in the woods, and tossing the heads away separately.

Kemper had now killed and dismembered six young women in the space of just over a year. Although the police at this stage had no leads in the case and did not regard him as a suspect, he sensed that they were closing in. An officer he knew, Sergeant Aluffi, had called at his house just days before, to question him about a weapon he owned, and Kemper also feared that his mother might have found some of the souvenirs he'd taken from his victims.

On April 20, 1973, Clarnell went out with friends for the evening and came home slightly tipsy. Kemper, by now increasingly paranoid, was lying awake when she got in. He had decided to murder his mother, to save her from the embarrassment of learning that he was the "Coed Killer."

After Clarnell retired to bed, he crept into her room holding a claw hammer which he used to bludgeon her to death. He then decapitated the corpse and placed the head on a mantel where he threw darts at it. He also cut out his mother's vocal cords and dropped them in the garbage disposal. But the machine couldn't break down the tough vocal tissue and ejected it back up into the sink. "That seemed appropriate," Kemper later said, "as much as she'd bitched and screamed and yelled at me over so many years."

Kemper knew now that the game was up and that he'd be arrested for his mother's murder. But his lust for killing was still not sated. He therefore placed a call to his mother's best friend, asking her to come over to the house urgently. The minute 59-year-old Sally Hallett entered, Kemper overpowered her and strangled her to death. Then he stripped her naked and beheaded her. He spent that night in the house performing depravities on the two corpses. The following morning, he fled in Sally Hallet's car.

Kemper drove east, leaving California and passing through Nevada and Utah, all the while tuned in to the radio, hoping to hear news that the bodies had been discovered. When no news came, he decided to initiate the discovery himself. Stopping at a phone booth in Pueblo, Colorado, he called the Santa Cruz Police Department and confessed to the murders of his mother and Sally Hallet. At first, police thought it was a crank call, but Kemper phoned back and asked to speak to a detective he knew. Then he waited patiently at the phone booth for officers to arrive and arrest him, one of the few instances where a serial killer has willingly surrendered himself to the authorities.

Once in custody, Kemper quickly confessed to the "Coed Killings," and led investigators to the remains of his victims. He went on trial in October 1973, charged with eight murders. On November 8, the jury deliberated for five hours before finding Kemper guilty on all counts. He asked for the death penalty but with the moratorium in place on capital punishment at the time, he was sentenced to life imprisonment without the possibility of parole.

Edmund Kemper is currently serving his term at California Medical Facility in Vacaville. He has stated on several occasions that he never wants to be released for fear that he will kill again.

Charles Albright

The Texas Eyeball Killer

When Mary Lou Pratt's nearly nude body was found in the Oak Cliff neighborhood of Dallas, Texas on December 13, 1990, Detective John Westphalen knew the chances of finding her killer were slim. Pratt was a known prostitute, operating in an area frequented by streetwalkers, pimps, and pushers. It was unlikely the murder had occurred here, and if anyone had seen the body being dumped, no one was saying. Same as it ever was.

The body was removed to the morgue, where the medical examiner, Dr. Elizabeth Peacock, conducted an autopsy to confirm the cause of death. Shooting was the obvious choice (the woman had a .44 slug buried in her skull) but she might have had been shot post-mortem - not likely, but possible. As Dr. Peacock pushed back the right eyelid, to examine the condition of the victim's eyes, she started. Even to an experienced M.E., this was unusual. There was a gaping hole behind the lid. Someone had removed the eyeball. Not only that, but it had been done with surgical care, and the left eye was the same. The killer had removed his victim's eyes and carried them away as a ghoulish trophy.

Gory though this detail was, it at least gave Detective Westphalen something to work with. He started by contacting the FBI's VICAP unit and requesting details of any other murders that might carry this unique signature. The search came up blank, but criminal behavioralists at the Bureau warned Westphalen that, given the highly ritualized nature of the crime, the killer was likely to strike again.

And so it proved. On February 10, 1991, two months after the first murder, the body of another prostitute was discovered. She was 27-year-old Susan Peterson, and she was found in a similar condition to Mary Lou Pratt, near nude, her T-shirt pulled up to display her breasts, bullet wounds to the back of the head, her eyes removed.

So now Dallas PD knew they had a repeat killer on their hands, one who was likely to kill again unless he was stopped. And given the area in which Peterson had been dumped (close to where Pratt's body had been found), it was likely that the killer was a local man, operating within his zone of familiarity. That being the case, the logical next step was to get on the ground and talk to the resident hookers.

Their questions turned up a couple of interesting leads. One prostitute described being beaten and almost killed by one of her johns and then stunned investigators by saying that she'd seen the same man kill Mary Lou Pratt. However, she was unable to provide any further details, and when local beat cops pointed out that she was a habitual liar, the lead petered out, as did other scant clues. The police beefed up patrols in the area and hoped they'd get their man before he struck again. They didn't.

On March 18, another murder occurred - and threw up another surprise for investigators. Serial killers tend to kill within their racial group, and given the race of the first two victims, detectives had assumed they were looking for a white man. But the latest victim, a 41-year-old prostitute named, Shirley Williams, was black. She was found lying on her side near a school, blood from her facial wounds pooled on the sidewalk. As with the other two victims, her eyes had been removed. But unlike the other two, this was a botched job. The victim's face had been slashed, and the tip of an X-Acto knife had been left behind in her eye socket. Perhaps, the killer had been rushed.

But not so rushed that he'd left behind any evidence, as before there was no semen, no fingerprints. However, there was one minuscule clue that the crime scene team was able to pick up – a single hair, found on the victim's neck. Placed under the microscope back at the lab, it turned out to be a pubic hair from a Caucasian - not much use in tracking the perpetrator, but useful for comparison once a suspect was identified.

And ballistics yielded another valuable piece of information. The gun that had killed Shirley Williams was the same one that had killed Mary Lou Pratt. This was important because the killer had botched the removal of Williams' eyes. A sharp defense attorney might suggest that the crime had been committed by a copycat.

In any murder investigation, investigators get hundreds of tip-offs. Most of them are useless, yet all but the most bizarre have to be followed up. And sometimes, just sometimes, a tip-off provides a valuable clue or a viable suspect. So it was in this case, when a frightened woman phoned in and gave investigators a name - Charles Albright.

The woman said she'd worked at a clothing store where Albright was a customer. He'd taken a liking to her and had started showering her with gifts. Eventually, against the advice of her co-workers who thought he was creepy, she agreed to go out with him. Although Albright was married, he convinced the woman to move into one of his rental properties and to become his lover. She soon had cause to regret her decision. Albright's sexual demands became weirder and weirder until she was convinced he was going to kill her. Eventually, she'd moved out, to get away from him. But years later she was still terrified that Albright might find her and kill her.

All of this was very interesting but it was the next flurry of information that put Albright firmly in the frame - his house was close to where the first victim had been found; he was acquainted with both Mary Lou Pratt and Susan Peterson; he had an obsession with knives...and with eyes.

Armed with this information, Detective Westphalen arranged to show a collection of mug shots to the prostitute who'd been attacked. She immediately picked out Charles Albright as the man who had assaulted her.

Detectives didn't have enough yet to bring Albright in for murder, but they did have him on assault and attempted murder. They decided to take him into custody while they strengthened their case. In the early hours of March 22, Albright was arrested at his home (he'd later complain about officers breaking into his house and using a stun grenade when all they had to do was knock).

Their main suspect now in custody, Dallas PD went about making their case. But a search of Albright's house turned up nothing incriminating. Police did find a red condom, similar to one found at one of the crime scenes, a collection of X-acto knives, like those used to remove the victims' eyes; and a stash of guns, including a .44 revolver, the caliber used in the murders (ballistics would later prove it wasn't the murder weapon).

And an interrogation of Albright's wife turned up further problems for investigators. Dixie Albright provided her husband with an alibi for all three murders. She also insisted that at the time of the murders Albright's car had been in the shop, so he'd have had no way of transporting the bodies.

Eventually, it was time for Westphalen to question Charles Albright. Unsurprisingly, he denied any involvement. He claimed that he didn't know any of the victims or any prostitutes for that matter. He admitted that he had previous convictions, but insisted they were all for property crimes. Confronted about a sexual assault he'd previously pled guilty to, Albright claimed he'd only admitted the charge to avoid the embarrassment of a trial.

The more the investigators talked to Albright, the more they began to think they'd acted too hastily in bringing him in. He certainly didn't fit the profile of a serial killer. He had a master's degree and spoke several languages; he was charming and articulate and in an apparently stable and satisfying relationship; he didn't do drugs; he was quite happy for investigators to search his home and run tests on his firearms. Moreover, at 57, he seemed too old – serial killers typically start killing in their twenties or thirties.

Digging below the surface, though, a different picture of Charles Albright emerged.

Charles was born on August 10, 1933, and adopted soon after by Delle and Fred Albright. Delle was an elementary school teacher and a strict disciplinarian. Yet, she doted on young Charles and was overprotective towards him. She also accelerated his education, tutoring him personally and helping him to skip two grades.

For his 13th birthday, Fred bought him a rifle and he took to shooting small animals. He then expressed an interest in taxidermy, and Delle encouraged this, teaching him how to skin and stuff his kills. The only concession that needed to be made was the eyes. They couldn't afford the expensive glass kind, so had to make do with buttons. Might this have been the root of Albright's eye obsession?

Although Albright excelled at his studies he was often in trouble, acquiring a juvenile record for petty theft and aggravated assault by the time he was 13. Still, in 1949, at the age of just 15, he'd acquired enough credits to graduate from high school and attend North Texas State University.

At 16, he was in trouble with the law again, charged with theft of cash and firearms. And this time, despite Delle's vigorous efforts on his behalf, he served jail time, a year in a juvenile detention center.

Released in 1950, he attended Arkansas State Teacher's College, majoring in pre-med studies. But Albright still hadn't learned his lesson. He was again found in possession of stolen property and although he wasn't charged, he was expelled from the school. Not that it fazed Charles Albright; he simply stole some blanks, forged some signatures, and awarded himself bachelor's and master's degrees.

Soon after, Albright married his college girlfriend and settled down to a seemingly normal life. But he never could hold a job and also hadn't lost his taste for forgery and petty thievery. Eventually, it caught up with him. Albright had been working as a science teacher (a good one by all accounts), but when it was discovered that his degree was forged, he was fired.

Things went from bad to worse in 1965 when his wife left him, taking their infant daughter with her. The couple would eventually divorce in 1974.

His marriage may have ended, but Albright's career as a petty criminal was still going full speed ahead. Caught stealing merchandise from a hardware store, he was sentenced to two years in prison.

The next traumatic event in Albright's life was the death of his adoptive mother Delle, in 1981, when Albright was 48. That same year, Albright was visiting some friends, when he was accused of sexually molesting their nine-year-old daughter. Albright pleaded guilty and got probation (later he'd claim he was innocent but had entered the plea to avoid a trial).

Albright was already visiting prostitutes regularly by now, his sexual appetites funded by the sizeable sum he'd inherited on the death of his father. Then, in 1985, he met Dixie and persuaded her to come and live with him. His intentions may not have been entirely romantic. Albright had quickly burnt through his inheritance; Dixie was soon paying all the bills. For all his intelligence and capabilities, at the time of his arrest, Albright was reduced to running a paper route.

The murder case seemed to be falling apart. Investigators had found nothing in Albright's house to link him to the murders, ballistics tests showed that none of his registered guns was the murder weapon and Dixie had provided garage receipts to prove that Albright was without a car when the killings had occurred.

There was, however, forensic evidence. Hairs found on a blanket in Albright's truck matched Shirley Williams, and the pubic hair found on Williams' body matched Albright. And there was circumstantial evidence; two prostitutes came forward to describe attacks by Albright, one of which had occurred in the field where Shirley Williams had been found. Then, a former confidant of Albright, told police that he had another .44 caliber revolver, registered in his father's name. Police were unable to find the weapon, but the fact that it was missing, was telling.

In the end, although it was far from the most watertight case, the D.A. decided to file capital murder charges against Albright. Given the paucity of evidence, the grand jury reduced the charge to murder, meaning that the death penalty would not be a consideration. The D.A. then decided to drop the Pratt and Peterson charges and to proceed only with the Shirley Williams charge, for which the prosecution had the most evidence.

Charles Albright's trial began on December 2, 1991, and lasted just over two weeks. On December 18, the jury deliberated for a full day before returning a guilty verdict. Albright was sentenced to a term of five years to life, a verdict upheld on a subsequent appeal.

In prison, Albright continues to protest his innocence. However, his obsession with eyes is plain for all to see. He subscribes to a magazine about iridology and one of his prized possessions is the first issue of Omni magazine, which features a large eyeball on the cover. A talented cartoonist, he spends much of his time doodling, decorating his cell with his creations. Almost without fail, they feature pictures of eyes.

Carl Panzram

"Hurry up, you Hoosier bastard, I could hang a dozen men while you're screwing around." the last words of Carl Panzram

Remorseless killer, child rapist, habitual, hate-filled criminal, Carl Panzram was all of these things and more. One of the most ferocious serial murderers in history, he began his criminal career at the age of eight. By 11 he was consigned to a brutal reform school where, for two years, he was regularly sodomized and viciously tortured and beaten.

That set the tone for the man Carl Panzram would become, a true misanthrope with a burning hatred for the human race. By his teens, Panzram was setting fires and fantasizing about committing mass murder. By the time he ran away from home and began riding the rails at 14, he was already hard as nails, with a loathing for everyone, including himself.

A wanderer by nature, Panzram crisscrossed the United States, burning, raping, and murdering as he went. This one-man crime wave even traveled to Europe, South America, and Africa, committing atrocities wherever he found himself.

Few prisons could hold him, and none - despite vicious beatings, torture, and starvation – could break him. He remained unbowed, unapologetic, defiant. "I have no desire to reform myself," he said in his autobiography. "My only desire is to reform people who try to reform me. And I believe that the only way to reform people is to kill them."

Carl Panzram was born on June 28, 1891, on a desolate farm near Warren, Minnesota. His parents were of German stock, hardworking, but like most other immigrants of that era, dirt poor. His father, Johan, deserted the family when Panzram was just seven, leaving a tremendous weight on his over-burdened mother, Matilda. The family worked the farm from sunup to sundown with very little to show for their efforts.

In 1899, Carl had his first brush with the law, dragged before a juvenile court on a drunk and disorderly charge, at the age of just eight. Soon his acts of petty thievery would land him at the Minnesota State Training School in Red Wing. Discipline here was rigid, even sadistic. The boys were made to work from dawn till dark and subjected to regular beatings. Sexual abuse was rife, from both guards and fellow inmates.

When Carl emerged from his sentence, in late 1905, he was a changed boy, brooding, withdrawn, and angry. By March the following year, he left the family farm for good, hopping a westbound freight train at East Grand Forks, North Dakota. Carl Panzram was about to be unleashed on the world.

Over the next few years, Panzram ranged across the Midwest, sleeping in freight cars, riding under trains, and doing his best to avoid the violent railroad cops. He begged for food and stole whatever and whenever he could.

Inevitably, he fell foul of the law. Arrested in Butte, Montana for burglary, he was sent to the Montana State Reform School at Miles City. Panzram was just 14, but he soon developed a reputation as a violent and difficult inmate. When a guard foolishly turned his back on the boy, Panzram bludgeoned him with a heavy wooden plank, earning himself a severe beating and a period of solitary confinement.

Not long after his release from solitary, Panzram escaped in the company of fellow inmate, Jimmie Benson. Over the next month, the duo robbed and rampaged their way through Montana. A favorite target of Panzram's was churches, which he'd burglarize and then burn to the ground.

After the pair went their separate ways, Panzram drifted to Helena, Montana, where he enlisted in the U.S. Army. It seems a strange career choice for Panzram, given his problems with authority. And so it proved, in trouble virtually from day one, he was eventually court marshaled for theft in April 1907, and sentenced to three years at Leavenworth.

Panzram was still only 16 years old when he arrived at the imposing federal prison in 1907. Over the next three years, he spent up to 14 hours a day, seven days a week, in all weather conditions, breaking rocks. He suffered numerous beatings for infractions as minor as speaking out of turn. By the time he emerged in 1910, he was an awesome sight to behold, six feet tall, lean and muscled from his physical labors, mean as spit.

He drifted down to Mexico where he joined up with the rebel leader Pascual Orozco, who served under Venustiano Carranza. Later, he returned to California and traveled the western seaboard, committing numerous robberies, assaults, and acts of sodomy. He'd later recall: "I have murdered twenty-one human beings. I have committed thousands of burglaries, robberies, larcenies, arson, and last but not least I have committed sodomy on more than 1,00 male human beings."

Panzram used numerous aliases during his criminal career, over the next few years he was arrested under the names 'Jefferson Baldwin', 'Jack Allen', and 'Jefferson Davis'. He showed up in Texas, Kansas, and California and escaped from jails in Rusk, Texas, and The Dalles, Oregon.

Eventually, the law caught up with him in Chinook, Montana. Sentenced to one year on a burglary charge, he escaped eight months later. A year later, he was back in the brig, this time serving two years on burglary charges, under the alias 'Jeff Rhodes.' Paroled in 1914, he was arrested for another burglary in Astoria, Oregon. This time, the sentence was seven years at the state prison in Salem. Not long after, a further seven years was added to his term after he attempted to incite a prison riot.

But, as always, Panzram had no intention of serving his sentence. He broke out in May 1918 and headed to Maryland, where he robbed a hotel in the town of Frederick, netting $1,200. Traveling from there to New York, Panzram signed on board the James Whitney, a merchant vessel bound for South America, but jumped ship in Peru to work in a copper mine.

He traveled to Chile where he worked for the Sinclair Oil Company at Bocas Del Toro. However, Panzram was never going to hold down a straight job for long. Always a keen pyromaniac, he set fire to an oil rig and fled. A $500 reward was posted, but Panzram evaded capture and slipped back undetected into the U.S.

In 1920, he showed up in Bridgeport, Connecticut, where he robbed a jewelry store, making off with $7,000. Later that summer he burglarized the residence of former US president, William Howard Taft in New Haven. Panzram made off with a considerable booty in jewels and liberty bonds. He also stole the former President's .45 Colt Army Automatic, which he'd soon put to use in a series of callous murders.

With his huge windfall from the Taft burglary, Panzram bought a yacht, the Akista, registering it under the alias 'John O'Leary.' He sailed to New York, navigating the East River, Long Island Sound, and the south shore of the Bronx.

Noticing a large number of sailors on shore leave, many of them looking for work, he cooked up another scheme. "I figured it would be a good plan to hire a few sailors to work for me, get them out to my yacht, get them drunk, commit sodomy on them, rob them, and then kill them."

Over the following weeks, Panzram put this fiendish plan into action. He would go down to the South Street neighborhood and pick out one or two victims, offering them work on his yacht. After working them for a day he'd ply them with booze, then shoot them and throw their weighted bodies overboard. He worked this scheme for about three weeks, but eventually, his actions attracted the attention of the locals, so he sailed further down the coast towards New Jersey. Here the Akista ran into a huge storm and was wrecked. Panzram and his deckhands swam for shore, the two sailors not realizing how lucky they'd been.

In 1921, Panzram served six months of jail time in Bridgeport, Connecticut, for burglary. On his release, he headed for Philadelphia where he became involved in a labor dispute. After a battle with strikebreakers, he was arrested again, but jumped bail and fled back to Connecticut. Here, he stowed away on a ship bound for Europe, and from there worked his way to Angola, a Portuguese colony on the west coast of Africa.

Panzram again found work with Sinclair Oil, but after hearing about the good money to be made hunting crocodiles, he hired a team of six African porters and headed up the Congo River. After a few days of successful hunting, the natives made the grave mistake of demanding a share of the profits. Panzram resolved the dispute by shooting all six men and feeding them to the hungry crocodiles.

Realizing that he'd been seen going into the jungle with the murdered men, Panzram realized that he had to get out of Angola. He worked his way back to Portugal, but here too, police were on the lookout for him. Managing to stow away on another ship, he made his way back across the Atlantic, arriving back in America in the summer of 1922.

Back on U.S. soil, Panzram went to the Customs office in New York, renewed his captain's license, and retrieved the papers for his yacht. His plan was to steal a vessel that was similar to the Akista, refit it, and register it as his own. He traveled from New York to Connecticut and Rhode Island without success, arriving eventually in the town of Salem, Massachusetts. Here, Panzram, waylaid, sodomized, and murdered a 12-year-old boy named Henry McMahon, clubbing him to death with a rock. Later he'd describe the incident by saying, "I tried a little sodomy on him first, then I left him laying there with his brains coming out of his ears."

After the McMahon murder, Panzram headed back to New York where he found work as a night watchman for the Abeeco Mill Company. The summer of 1923 found him back in Providence, Rhode Island, where he eventually found the boat he was looking for. After stealing the yawl from a marina, he sailed for Long Island Sound. At Yonkers, he picked up a 15-year-old boy, George Walsoin, who he took on board as a deckhand.

The pair sailed 50 miles up the Hudson River to Kingston where Panzram repainted the ship's hull and changed the name on the stern. He then went on shore to find a buyer for the boat. The interested party, though, turned out to be a criminal himself. That night he tried to sneak on board and Panzram killed him, shooting him twice in the head.

Panzram threw the body overboard and fled the jurisdiction. But at Newburgh, George Walsoin dived overboard and swam to shore. He made his way to a police station and informed officers that he'd been sexually assaulted. He also told them about the killing of the would-be robber.

Police put out an alert for Panzram and arrested him at Nyack on the morning of June 29, 1923. Charged with sodomy, robbery, and burglary Panzram convinced his lawyer to post bail for him, promising that he'd hand over his boat in payment. The minute the bond was posted, he fled. When the lawyer tried to register the yacht, he found it was stolen.

Panzram, meanwhile, moved back to Connecticut, where, on August 9, 1923, he raped and strangled another twelve-year-old boy, tossing his body into some bushes beside a busy road. Panzram then hopped a freight train headed for Manhattan. In New York, he found work on a steamer that was due to sail for China. However, even before the ship embarked he was fired for brawling with his crewmates.

He next showed up in the village of Larchmont, New York where he was arrested for breaking into a railway station and trying to steal luggage. In custody, Panzram inexplicably confessed to several other burglaries as well as to being a fugitive from an Oregon prison.

Panzram was sent to Sing Sing on a 5-year sentence for burglary. When the guards at that facility were unable to control him, he was transferred to Clinton Penitentiary in Dannemora, considered the most brutal, repressive prison in America.

Even here, among the toughest of the tough, the inmates other prisons had given up on, Panzram stood out. In short order, he firebombed a workshop and attacked one of the guards. These earned him severe punishments, beatings, and solitary. Within a few months, he tried to escape but broke both his legs and ankles in the attempt. No medical attention was given. He was simply thrown onto the cold floor of his cell and left there. Over 14 excruciating months, his legs did eventually heal, but he was left with a permanent limp.

Not that it slowed down Carl Panzram. Released from Clinton in 1928, he unleashed his anger on the Baltimore-Washington, D.C. area, committing eleven burglaries and at least,one murder there, leading to his arrest on August 16, 1928.

While in prison in D.C. a 26-year-old rookie guard by the name of Henry Lesser took pity on Panzram. Reportedly, Lesser gave Panzram a dollar to buy cigarettes, coaxing a tear from the tough as rawhide prisoner. Panzram said it was the first kindness anyone had shown him in his entire life.

Following this incident, Lesser befriended Panzram and convinced him to write his life story. The guard provided the writing implements and Panzram spewed out a hate-filled missive detailing his misdeeds and his hatred for the human race.

Panzram's trial for the burglary and housebreaking charges opened on November 12, 1928. He served as his own attorney and spent the session intimidating jurors, jurists, and witnesses. Sentenced to twenty-five years in Leavenworth, he left with a defiant word for the judge "Visit me!" he shouted.

Back in Leavenworth, twenty years after he'd first been incarcerated there, Panzram issued a grim warning to the deputy warden, "I'll kill the first man who bothers me."

He was good to his word too. On June 20, 1929, less than five months after he'd arrived, Panzram attacked a civilian employee, Robert G. Warnke, his supervisor in the laundry room. Warnke was a small balding man, known for writing prisoners up on minor infractions. Panzram had previously told other prisoners that he was going to kill Warnke. On the day of the murder, Warnke was filling out some paperwork when Panzram picked up a metal bar and, without a word, crossed the room to where Warmke sat. He raised the bar above his head and crashed it down onto Warmke's head, then kept bludgeoning him until nothing remained but a bloody pulp. Then he turned his attention on the other prisoners, injuring several of them before guards arrived with machine guns to subdue him.

Panzram went on trial for the murder of Robert Warnke on April 14, 1930. Unsurprisingly, he was found guilty and sentenced to die on the gallows. He seemed pleased with the sentence, thanking the judge and stating that he had no intention of appealing. When the Society for the Abolishment of Capital Punishment petitioned the governor for a pardon or a commutation of sentence, Panzram sent them a threatening letter, promising to kill them all if he was reprieved and got out of prison.

He went to the gallows on September 5, 1930. Defiant to the last, he spat in the executioner's face, then growled: "Hurry up you Hoosier bastard, I could kill ten men while you're screwing around!"

Loren Herzog & Wesley Shermantine Jr.

The Speed Freak Killers

Loren Herzog and Wes Shermantine grew up together on the same street in the small farming community of Linden, California. Virtually inseparable as children the two buddies spent their time doing what other kids did, hanging out, playing ball, and, in their case, exploring the hills, ravines, and mineshafts around their hometown. Wes' father was a successful contractor, fond of indulging his son with anything his heart desired. An avid hunter and fisherman, Shermantine Sr. would often take the boys with him, teaching them how to cast and how to shoot. It was an idyllic childhood.

But as the boys grew older, troubling signs began to emerge. By high school, they were notorious bullies and troublemakers, heavy drinkers, and eventually, habitual users of hard drugs, particularly methamphetamine (or speed). When they moved into an apartment together, their drug-taking escalated and they began roaming the highways and bi-ways of San Joaquin County, terrorizing anyone they encountered. They also took to killing people for kicks.

It is impossible to determine when the deadly duo killed their first victim, but investigators who worked their case believe it may have been the murder of Chevelle 'Chevy' Wheeler in 1985.

On Wednesday, October 16, 1985, Chevy Wheeler, a 16-year-old from Stockton, California told some of her classmates at Franklin High School that she was cutting classes to go with a male friend to Valley Springs. She seemed somewhat uneasy about making the trip and told a friend that, if she didn't return that day, the friend should tell her father where she'd gone. She was last seen getting into a red pickup outside the school premises.

When Chevy didn't return, the friend, as agreed, informed Mr. Wheeler. He immediately called the police. Authorities soon learned that the friend Chevy had agreed to accompany to Valley Springs was Wesley Shermantine, 19 years old, and well known to them as a drug user and troublemaker. Shermantine was acquainted with the Wheeler family, and police also noted that he owned a red pickup truck like the one Chevy had been seen getting into. Chevy's family also told police that Shermantine had called at their home on the morning of Chevy's disappearance.

Armed with this information, detectives pulled Shermantine in for questioning. He denied any knowledge of her whereabouts or any involvement in her disappearance. Yet, even as he protested his innocence to Chevy's family, detectives sensed that he was lying.

They learned that Shermantine was staying at a cabin his family owned in San Andreas, California, and obtained a search warrant for the premises, where they found blood and hair evidence. However, although the blood matched Chevy's blood type, it was not enough to bring charges against Shermantine. The DNA-testing technology of the time was not advanced enough to make a conclusive match. The evidence went into storage where it would remain for 14 years before it would come back to haunt Wesley Shermantine.

Over a decade later, on Friday, November 13, 1998, Cyndi Vanderheiden spent the evening with friends at the Linden Inn, a karaoke bar in Linden, California. Also in attendance that night, were Herzog and Shermantine, who Cyndi spoke with for a time. Eventually, Cyndi and her friends decided to leave, and, as she'd had quite a lot to drink, one of them drove her car, stopping off at the Old Corner Saloon in Clements. This bar was just a mile from where Cyndi lived with her parents, so when they left a while later, she said she was okay to drive. Nonetheless, one of her male friends followed her home, to see that she made it okay. The man saw her park in the driveway at approximately 2:30 a.m. but did not wait around until she went into the house.

Cyndi's mother would later tell investigators that she had heard her daughter pull into the drive but had then dozed off again and hadn't heard her enter the house. The following morning, Cindy was nowhere to be found. Her bed had not been slept in and her car wasn't in the garage or the driveway. As Cindy's worried father began driving the streets of the town looking for her, he came across her car parked outside Glenview Cemetery. The car was unlocked, and Cindy's purse and cell phone were inside. With growing concern, Mr. Vanderheiden searched the cemetery grounds and then called the police.

But a police search was no more successful in finding the missing girl than her father's had been. It was speculated that Cyndi had parked in her parent's driveway for a short while and then, rather than going into the house, she'd driven out to the cemetery. But for what reason? And where was she now?

Despite the police searches and the subsequent investigation, those questions appeared to have no answers. And they might have remained a mystery had officers working a cold case not submitted their old evidence for reanalysis.

Since the murder of Chevy Wheeler in 1985, there had been significant advances in DNA technology. The blood and hair samples gathered from Shermantine's cabin were sent to the crime lab again. Soon after, there was a match. The blood and hair were from Chevy Wheeler.

Detectives had long believed Wes Shermantine to be the perpetrator and they now moved in to arrest him. Shermantine was taken into custody on March 18, 1999. He denied killing Chevy, claiming his friend Loren Herzog had committed the crime. Herzog had a key to the cabin, he said, and had been friends with Chevy.

Faced with the accusations, Herzog flatly denied them. He told officers that Shermantine had bragged to him about killing Chevy. Then he dropped a bombshell. Not only had Wes killed Chevy Wheeler, he'd also killed Cyndi Vanderheiden. And, hinted Herzog, there were other murders, too.

The officers were stunned, but not entirely surprised to hear Shermantine's name mentioned in connection with the Vandermeiden murder. However, they were not prepared to accept Herzog's assertion that he had no involvement in the murder. After all, the two were always together, and Herzog's reputation was equal to Shermantine's in depravity. Over the next 17 hours, San Joaquin County Sheriff's detectives interrogated Loren Herzog mercilessly, recording most of the interview on videotape.

According to Herzog, Shermantine was a serial killer, involved in at least five unsolved murders in northern California, and one in Utah. He (Herzog) had witnessed all of the murders but hadn't actively participated in any of them.

The first murder had happened in 1984, he said. They'd been driving a truck along Highway 88 in the area of Hope Valley, California when they'd passed a vehicle pulled to the side of the road. The driver was intoxicated and had pulled over to sober up. Shermantine had pulled up beside him and got out of the truck. Then, without provocation or warning, he'd shot the man with a shotgun. The driver would later be identified as Henry Howell, 41, a resident of Santa Clara, California.

Two months later, Herzog said, they were driving on Roberts Island, southwest of Stockton, when they passed a 1982 Pontiac. Shermantine had turned his truck around and stopped next to the Pontiac. He and Herzog got out, both carrying shotguns. Shermantine shot the driver, 35-year-old, Howard King, while he sat behind the wheel. They then dragged the passenger, Paul Cavanaugh, 31, from the vehicle and Shermantine shot him as he begged for his life. Witnesses at the time had reported seeing a red pickup truck in the area and tire tracks found at the scene were later matched to the tires on Shermantine's pickup.

In September of the following year, Herzog and Shermantine met Robin Armtrout, 24, at a park in Stockton. They agreed to go out drinking together but drove instead to a field outside Linden. At some point, Shermantine had begun beating the young woman and had then raped her before stabbing her to death. Her nude body was later found by a hunter. A witness had seen her getting into a red pickup with two men.

Herzog said Shermantine had later boasted about doing the same thing to Chevy Wheeler.

Of the Cyndi Vanderheiden murder, Herzog said he and Shermantine had arranged to meet Cyndi at the Glenview Cemetery under the pretense of giving her some speed. Cyndi had done drugs with Herzog and Shermantine previously. The three had met up at the cemetery, leaving Cyndi's car there while they drove back to Linden in

Shermantine's pickup. While they were driving Shermantine pulled a knife and ordered Cyndi to perform oral sex on him. He then stopped the truck, and raped Cyndi, before slashing her throat. At least some of this story checked out. Cyndi had been seen talking to the two men at the Linden Inn and her blood was found on the passenger-side headrest and inside the trunk of Shermantine's car.

But Herzog wasn't done yet. He also implicated Shermantine in the 1994 shooting of a hunter in northern Utah. Police there confirmed that the murder had occurred and was still unsolved.

So far, detectives had heard Loren Herzog's side of the story. Now, they played the videotape of the confession to Wes Shermantine. Upon hearing Herzog's statement, Shermantine immediately denied his involvement, insisting that Herzog had killed Cyndi. He added that Herzog could lead police to Cyndi's body.

As the former friends turned on each other and traded accusations, investigators were left to wonder which one, if either, was telling the truth. One thing did bother them, though. According to both of their statements, they'd killed five people before they were 21, then they'd killed nobody else for over a decade. That just didn't ring true.

Especially as Shermantine was often heard to brag that he'd "disappeared" 19 people. He's also allegedly once pushed a woman's head to the ground during a confrontation and told her to, "listen to the heartbeats of people I've buried here. Listen to the heartbeats of families I've buried here."

Shermantine went on trial on November 22, 2000, in Santa Clara. He continued to protest his innocence but was found guilty of the murders of Chevy Wheeler, Cyndi Vanderheiden, Paul Cavanaugh, and Howard King. He received the death penalty for these crimes and currently awaits execution at California's San Quentin prison. In the years since his sentencing, he has offered to point out the location of various bodies in exchange for cash. His offers have always been declined.

Herzog's trial took place in August 2001 for the murders of Cyndi Vanderheiden, Howard King, Paul Cavanaugh, Robin Armtrout, and Henry Howell. He was found not guilty of killing Robin Armtrout and Henry Howell, but guilty of the first-degree murders of Cyndi Vanderheiden, Howard King III, and Paul Cavanaugh. Herzog was sentenced to 78 years in prison. However, these convictions were overturned in August 2004, after it was found that police had improperly interrogated him.

Over the protests of residents and politicians, Loren Herzog was freed under strict parole conditions in July 2010. Just over 18 months later, on January 16, 2012, he was found dead in his trailer. Herzog had hung himself, leaving behind a suicide note that read, "Tell my family I love them."

A month after Herzog's death, Shermantine provided maps to five burial sites which he claimed were Herzog's "bone yards." Here police found the remains of Cyndi Vanderheiden and Chevelle Wheeler as well as over 1,000 other human bone fragments.

Randy Kraft

The Scorecard Killer

In the early hours of May 14, 1983, two California Highway Patrolmen pulled over a suspected drunk driver on the San Diego Freeway, near Mission Viejo. The driver staggered from his vehicle, discarding a beer bottle as he did. He insisted he was sober, although a field sobriety test proved otherwise. The officers then placed the man, identified as 38-year-old Randy Steven Kraft, of Long Beach, under arrest for driving under the influence.

It looked like a routine DUI but as Sgt. Michael Howard approached Kraft's Toyota Celica, he saw another man slumped over in the passenger's seat. The man's pants were unzipped, his genitals exposed. Howard rapped on the window and got no response. He then opened the car door and tried to rouse the man by shaking him – nothing. Howard placed his fingers to the man's throat and detected no pulse. He did, however, notice red marks on the man's neck, a clear sign of strangulation.

A murder suspect now, Kraft was taken into custody. But the evening's gruesome discoveries were not done yet. Among the discarded beer bottles, the supply of prescription painkillers, and the dried blood in Kraft's vehicle, police discovered a stash of macabre Polaroids, showing 47 nude young men, all of whom appeared to be either dead or unconscious. And in the trunk, they found a clue as to what they were dealing with - a notepad with 61 perplexing entries, that detectives soon realized was a list of murder victims.

Already reeling from the recent arrests of "Trash Bag Killer" Patrick Kearney and "Freeway Killer" William Bonin, California had another serial killer on its hands. And, if the numbers were correct, Randy Kraft had claimed more victims than Kearney and Bonin combined.

Randy Kraft was born on March 19, 1945, in Long Beach, California, the youngest child, and only son, of Harold and Opal Kraft, Wyoming natives who had moved west just the year before. In 1948, the family moved to Midway City, in Orange County. The community was conservative and the young Randy seems to have absorbed this attitude into his own worldview. His high school classmates remember him as being ultra-right wing, and he carried these views with him into his first year of college. He was, for example, a vocal supporter of the Vietnam War, and a tireless campaigner for conservative presidential candidate Barry Goldwater, in 1964.

The following year, though, brought a radical change to the straight-laced Randy. He grew his hair, cultivated a mustache, and got a part-time job as a barman in a gay bar. Rumors started to circulate campus of his fondness for bondage and he began consuming copious amounts of Valium (to ward off headaches caused by a childhood fall, he said).

In 1966, he moved off campus and set up house with a male friend in Huntington Beach. He also began to spend all of his free time in gay bars and acquired his first arrest – for lewd conduct – after propositioning an undercover police officer.

Despite a less than diligent application to his studies, Kraft graduated in 1968 with a bachelor's degree in economics. Soon after, he immersed himself in another political campaign, working so diligently for Robert Kennedy that he received a personal letter of thanks from the senator. He was devastated when Kennedy was assassinated. Just days later, he joined the U.S. Air Force and was posted to Edwards Air Force Base, where he would eventually supervise the painting of test planes.

A year later, in 1969, Kraft stunned his family by telling them he was gay. Then, after his discharge from the military on "medical grounds," he resumed his bartending career and fully embraced the gay lifestyle. "There's a part of me that you will never know," Kraft told friends who were perplexed by the change in him. A part that was, no doubt, already fantasizing about killing. Soon he would start turning those fantasies into reality.

On October 5, 1971, police found a decomposing corpse alongside the Ortega Highway, in Orange County. The body turned out to be that of Wayne Joseph Dukette, a 30-year-old bartender at the Stables gay bar in Long Beach, who had been reported missing two weeks earlier. The coroner fixed his date of death at around September 20 but found nothing to indicate foul play. He was wrong. Wayne Dukette was Randy Kraft's first victim. The entry "STABLE" on Kraft's scorecard is believed to refer to Dukette.

Fifteen months later, on December 26, 1972, a motorist traveling the 405 Freeway near Seal Beach, spotted a nude body lying at the side of the road. The motorist alerted the police, who discovered the corpse of Edward Daniel Moore, a 20-year-old Marine based at Camp Pendleton. Moore had left the barracks on Christmas Eve. He'd been strangled, bludgeoned, and tossed from a moving car. There were clear signs of torture on the body, including bite marks on the genitals. A sock had been jammed up the victim's rectum.

The next body was discovered beside the Terminal Island Freeway, on February 6, 1973. The victim, who has never been identified, was estimated to be in his late teens or early twenties. And police had the first indications of a pattern. As in the murder of Edward Moore, a sock had been forced into the man's anus.

If this was a series, the killer was escalating. On Easter Sunday, police made another grim discovery, this time in Huntington Beach. The corpse was fully dressed, although barefooted. Underneath his bloody slacks, his genitals had been hacked away. Ligature marks on his wrists suggested that the injury may have been inflicted before death.

The mutilation of the next victim was even more severe. The corpse was dismembered and scattered across two counties: the head found in Long Beach; the torso, right leg, and both arms in San Pedro; the left leg in Sunset Beach. There were rope marks on the wrists and evidence that the corpse had been refrigerated before disposal.

And still, the death toll kept mounting. Ron Wiebe, a 20-year-old from Fullerton, vanished on July 28, 1973. He was found next to the 405 Freeway in Seal Beach, beaten and strangled, with bite marks on his stomach and penis and a sock shoved into his rectum.

Then, 23-year-old art student Vincent Cruz Mestas was found in a ravine in the San Bernardino Mountains on December 29, 1973. His hands were missing, and plastic sandwich bags covered the bloody stumps. A pencil had been forced into his penis prior to death.

Six months later, 20-year-old Malcolm Eugene Little was found propped up against a mesquite tree beside Highway 86, in Imperial County. His genitals had been severed and a tree branch had been rammed six inches into his rectum.

Another U.S. Marine fell prey to the killer three weeks later. Roger Dickerson, 18, was found near a golf club in Laguna Beach. He'd been strangled and sodomized and there were bite marks on his genitals.

August brought two more gruesome discoveries, 25-year-old Thomas Paxton Lee, known around Long Beach as a gay street hustler, and, 23-year-old Gary Wayne Cordova. Neither victim had been mutilated and the murders were not initially connected to the unknown killer.

There was little doubt about the next discovery, though. James Dale Reeves was found in Irvine on November 29, 1974. The killer posed the body with legs spread, a tree limb four feet long and three inches in diameter protruding from the anus.

In December 1974, John Leras, a 17-year-old high school student, was found floating in the surf at Sunset Beach, a wooden surveyor's stake hammered into his rectum. Leras had been strangled while bound. Two sets of footprints leading from the car park to the water seemed to indicate that two killers had been involved.

Three weeks later, on January 17, 1975, construction workers found 21-year-old Craig Victor Jonaites strangled to death alongside the Pacific Coast Highway, near Long Beach. He had not been mutilated, but the presence of alcohol and Valium in his blood suggested that he might have fallen prey to the same killer.

By now, there'd been fourteen brutal murders of young men in a little over three years, and yet the police had nothing. Not only that, but the killer appeared to be accelerating. Something had to be done to stop him.

On January 24, 1975, a week after the discovery of the latest victim, detectives from several jurisdictions met in Santa Ana, to organize a task force. Also present was a profiler from the FBI's Behavioral Science Unit, a special investigator from the California State Attorney General's office, and several forensic psychologists. Yet a re-examination of the various crimes turned up no significant leads. The killer was clever, careful, and resourceful. And he was still killing.

On March 29, 1975, friends of 19-year-old Keith Daven Crotwell, saw him hitch a ride with a black-and-white Mustang in Long Beach. Crotwell was not seen again until May 8 when three boys found his severed head near the Long Beach Marina. Police traced the registration of the Mustang and questioned its owner, Randy Kraft, on May 19. Kraft admitted giving Crotwell a ride but said he had dropped him off at an all-night café. With no evidence to suggest otherwise, the police were forced to release him without charge.

The interrogation by police might have unsettled Kraft because he took a 24-week break before he killed again. Larry Gene Walters, 21, was murdered in Los Angeles County on Halloween, 1975. Two months later, 22-year-old Mark Hall disappeared from a New

Year's Eve party, in San Juan Capistrano. His nude corpse was found on January 3, 1976, in the Cleveland National Forest. He'd been sodomized and tortured before death: his legs slashed with a broken bottle; his eyes, face, chest, and genitals burned with a cigarette lighter; a cocktail swizzle stick jammed through his penis into his bladder; his genitals severed and stuffed into his rectum. The medical examiner was able to deduce that the victim had been alive throughout much of the ordeal.

At around this time, Randy Kraft split with his long-time lover Jeff Graves, and moved into a Laguna Beach apartment with 19-year-old Jeff Seelig. And police were suddenly confronted with a new spate of murders, nine slayings confirmed in 1976, all of them teenagers, their bodies dismembered and discarded beside highways and in dumpsters. The task team was baffled. Was this a different killer, or had the man they'd been seeking changed his M.O. and victim type?

Further complicating matters, was the arrest of "Trashbag Killer" Patrick Kearney in 1977. At first, authorities thought Kearney was responsible for Kraft's murders, even though their M.O.'s were significantly different. Kearney's victims were all shot in the head, and he seemed offended by suggestions that he had used torture.

Kraft, secure in his new relationship with Jeff Seelig, had taken a break from murder. Seelig would later tell investigators that although he and Kraft regularly picked up hitchhikers for threesomes, he had never seen Kraft display any tendency towards violence.

Whether that is true or not, the beast inside Randy Kraft emerged again on April 16, 1978, when he picked up 19-year-old Marine, Scott Michael Hughes. Hughes was found the following day beside the 91 Freeway in Orange County. He'd been strangled to death, his genitals mutilated with a knife, one of his testicles removed.

Two months later, 23-year-old Roland Young was found stabbed to death, his genitals mutilated. Young had just been released from the Orange County jail on a charge of public intoxication. A week after the murder of Roland Young, Kraft murdered another Marine. Twenty-three-year-old Richard Keith was hiking back to Camp Pendleton when he crossed paths with the killer. His body was found by an off-duty fireman the next day.

The next victim was Keith Klingbeil, found by a motorist on the 1-5 near Mission Viejo on July 6, 1978. Klingbeil was still alive but died at the scene while paramedics fought to save his life. Then, Michael Joseph Inderbeiten, a 21-year-old Long Beach truck driver, was found, emasculated and sodomized, his eyelids seared with an automobile cigarette lighter.

On June 16, 1979, motorists traveling the 405 Freeway in Irvine were stunned to see a man pushed from a moving vehicle. He was another young Marine, Donald Harold Crisel and there were ligature marks on his neck and wrists. Death, though, was from an overdose of booze and painkillers.

As the body count continued to spiral, gay bars throughout southern California began posting warnings for their customers. It did nothing to stop the slaughter, over a dozen male corpses, ranging in age from 13 to 24, were found littering the freeways in 1979.

Neither was Randy Kraft confining his activities to California anymore. As a freelance data-processing consultant, he traveled extensively during this period, taking in Michigan, Oregon, New York, and Florida. He also traveled to Mexico and spent time in San

Diego and Lake Tahoe. And wherever he went corpses seemed to turn up.

Michael Sean O'Fallon, a 17-year-old Colorado native, was killed in Oregon in 1980, his murder bearing all the hallmarks of Kraft's work. Then, on September 3, 1980, children playing near El Toro Marine Airbase found the corpse of 19-year-old U.S. Marine, Robert Loggins. Another victim, Michael Duane Cluck, 17, was killed in April 1981, while hitchhiking from California to Oregon.

On July 29, 1981, residents of Echo Park, in Los Angeles, complained to police about a rank odor coming from the nearby Hollywood Freeway. Officers investigated and found two corpses. Thirteen-year-old Raymond Davis had disappeared while searching for a lost dog; 16-year-old Robert Avila, had gone missing from Hollywood weeks before. Three weeks later, 17-year-old Christopher Williams was found dead beside a road in the San Bernardino Mountains.

1982 brought more murders, 26-year-old Brian Whitcher, along the I-5 near Portland on November 26, Dennis Alt and Chris Schoenborn in Grand Rapids, Michigan, on December 7, while Kraft was in town for a computer conference. Their corpses were found together in Plainfield Township two days later, both doped with booze and Valium, then strangled. Schoenborn had a ballpoint pen from Kraft's hotel thrust into his bladder through his penis. Kraft gave the murders the designation "GR2" on his scorecard.

Two more men turned up in Oregon in December, but by now police had picked up on the similarities in the Oregon and California murders. They requested airline passenger records for the L.A. to Portland route - Randy Kraft's name appeared 18 times.

Before they could follow up the lead, though, Kraft had been arrested with the corpse in his passenger seat.

The killer was in custody, now began the job of ensuring that he would never be free to kill again, and the starting point for prosecutors was the list, the "scorecard," that had been found in Kraft's car.

This consisted of two neatly printed columns, 30 items on the left side, 31 on the right. It began with "STABLE" and ended with "WHAT YOU GOT." In between were clues like, "2 IN 1 HITCH," "GR2," "PORTLAND BLOOD," and "JAIL OUT." Some were obvious references to specific murders, others more difficult to decipher. Whatever their meaning, it seemed clear that at least 61 incidents were being referenced in a unique and macabre scorecard, documenting Randy Kraft's decade-long career as a sadistic serial murderer.

Kraft wasn't talking, though, he insisted that the list was entirely innocent, a catalog of sexual encounters with gay lovers. However, his Polaroid collection, showing many of the murder victims in poses that suggested they were already dead, was more difficult to explain.

More than five years after his arrest, Kraft's much-delayed trial finally came to court on September 26, 1988. Thirteen months and $10 million later, it concluded with a guilty verdict on 16 charges of capital murder. On August 11, 1989, the jury recommended the death penalty and Judge McCartin made it official on November 29, sentencing Kraft to die in California's gas chamber.

As at the time of writing, Randy Kraft awaits his execution on death row at San Quentin State Prison.

What Makes A Serial Killer?

"I don't march to the same drummer you do." – Convicted killer Douglas Clark a.k.a. The Sunset Strip Slayer

What makes a serial killer? Is there something unique in their genetic make-up, their physiology, thought patterns, or upbringing? Do they lack morality or social programming? Are they unable to control their rage and sexual urges? Are they mad or bad? What sets them apart?

These questions have vexed criminologists, profilers, psychologists, and forensic psychiatrists for decades. They've been the subject of countless studies and dissertations. They've formed the basis of thousands of man-hours worth of interviews and investigation. And yet, definitive answers remain elusive.

Serial killers themselves have offered some suggestions. Henry Lee Lucas blamed his upbringing; Jeffrey Dahmer said that he was born with a part of him missing; Ted Bundy blamed pornography; Herbert Mullin said it was voices in his head ordering him to kill; Kenneth Bianchi blamed an alter-ego, while Bobby Joe Long said a motorcycle accident turned him into a serial sex killer. Some, like John Wayne Gacy, even had the temerity to blame their victims.

As for the rest of us, we console ourselves that they must be insane. After all, what sane person could slaughter another for pleasure? What normal person could perpetuate the atrocities that serial killers do, and repeat them again and again?

Yet the most terrifying thing about serial killers is that they are not shambling, jabbering ogres, but rational and calculating, impossible to tell from the general populace until it's too late.

So what exactly is a serial killer?

The National Institutes of Justice defines serial murder as:

"A series of two or more murders committed as separate events, usually, but not always, by one offender acting alone. The crimes may occur over a period of time, ranging from hours to years. Quite often the motive is psychological, and the offender's behavior and the physical evidence observed at the crime scene will reflect sadistic sexual overtones."

And the FBI's Behavioral Science Unit provides us with some traits common in serial killers.

- They are typically white males in their twenties and thirties.

- They are usually quite smart, with an IQ designated, "bright normal."
- Despite their intelligence, they are underachievers, often doing poorly at school, and ending up in unskilled employment.
- They often come from broken homes with an absent father and a domineering mother. Some are adopted. Often, there is a history of psychiatric problems, criminality, and substance abuse in their families.
- Many were physically, psychologically, and/or sexually abused in childhood. Some have suffered head trauma due to abuse or an accident.
- In adolescence, many of them wet the bed, started fires, and tortured animals.
- They have problems with male authority figures and strong hostility towards women.
- They manifest psychological problems at an early age. Many have spent time in institutions as children.
- They have a general hatred towards humanity, including themselves. Some report suicidal thoughts as teenagers.
- They display an interest in sex at an unnaturally young age. As they mature this interest becomes obsessive and turns towards fetishism, voyeurism, and violent pornography.

A Façade of Normality

The traits listed above might incline you to believe that you'd be able to spot a serial killer a mile off, but the frightening truth is that they are masters at camouflage, deceit, and deception. They know exactly how to blend in, how to avert your suspicions, how to put you at ease. They are the charming stranger who strikes up a conversation with you on the bus, the lost driver who courteously asks for directions, the man hobbling on a cane who politely asks for your help.

Like all skilled predators, they can sniff out the slightest hint of an opportunity, they know who to target and how to stalk. Being psychologically vacant they are adept at assuming whatever role they need, and that role will be the one required to snare their victim. To quote serial killer, Henry Lee Lucas, "It's like being a movie star... you're just playing the part."

Is serial murder a recent phenomenon?

Since we're trying to understand what makes a serial killer, this is a valid question, and the answer depends on who you're listening to because there are two distinct schools of thought. One believes that societal influences since just before the turn of the 20th century (and especially since WWII) have created the perfect conditions for the emergence of serial killers. They point to serial killers as a symptom of crowded rat syndrome, a product of class struggle, and a manifestation of our attitudes toward sex.

The only problem with this argument is that it suggests that serial killers are purely a product of their environment. I consider that unlikely and am more inclined towards the second hypothesis, which holds that serial killers have always lived among us.

Adherents to this belief point to acts of human barbarism throughout history, from the terrible legends that appear in folklore, to the crimes of Gilles de Rais and Elizabeth Bathory, to the vicious outlaws and desperados of the Old West. They regard tales of werewolves, vampires, and man-eating trolls, as attempts by our less sophisticated ancestors to make sense of the hideous crimes committed by historical serial killers. A number of these legendary monsters, like the German "werewolf" Peter Stubbe and his French counterpart, Gilles Garnier, were captured and put to death. They proved to be, not lycanthropes, but all too human monsters, serial killers, in fact.

What makes a serial killer?

No single cause will ever provide an answer as to why serial killers are driven to commit murder again and again. Rather a combination of factors, physiological, psychological, and environmental, must be in play. Nonetheless, we can look at the known commonalities in captured serial killers and draw some conclusions. Is this a comprehensive list? Hardly. We simply lack the knowledge to solve the enigma of the serial killer.

Psychopaths

All serial killers, except perhaps for the small minority that are genuinely psychotic, are psychopaths. They would not be able to commit their horrendous crimes otherwise. Psychopaths are characterized by their irrationally antisocial behavior, their lack of conscience, their emotional emptiness, and their appetite for risk, all of which could easily be applied to serial killers.

Lacking empathy, they have no problem turning their victims into objects, there to be exploited and manipulated. Being devoid of emotions (in the way that you and I would understand them) they are like a blank screen, onto which can be projected whatever suits their needs in the moment. This is what makes them so good at play-acting and manipulation.

Being compulsive thrill seekers, they are literally fearless, sometimes abducting victims in broad daylight, or with a clear risk of discovery. This thrill-seeking behavior also means that they are less easily stimulated than normal people. They require higher levels of excitement to get their rocks off, even if it means murder and mayhem.

Does this mean that all psychopaths become serial killers? Absolutely not. Most psychopaths aren't even criminals. In fact, many excel in fields like business and political leadership. Not all psychopaths are serial killers, but all serial killers, most certainly, are psychopaths.

Sexual Deviance

A second factor that must be present in all serial killers is sexual deviance. Serial murders are by their nature, sex crimes. A sexual motive is a requisite in both the Institutes of Justice and FBI definitions and an examination of any serial murder (even those that appear to have a different motive) will undoubtedly prove that the killer achieved some form of sexual release in the commission of the crime.

According to Ressler, Burgess, and Douglas in Sexual Homicide: Patterns and Motives, there are two types of sexual homicide: "the rape or displaced anger murder" and the "sadistic, or lust murder."

For some murderers, rape is the primary objective for the crime, the murder committed to cover it up. For others, the act of murder and the ritual acts associated with it, provide the sexual release. The annals of serial murder abound with such cases, Bundy, Kearney, Kemper, Nilsen, and others were necrophiles; Rader, Kraft, Berdella et al. achieved sexual release through torture; others like Kroll and Fish, through cannibalism. Still others are aroused by stabbing or by the "intimate" act of strangulation.

And with serial killers, this deviance usually manifests in childhood. Fledgling serial killers are often flashers, peeping toms, molesters of younger children, chronic masturbators, even, as in the case of Harvey Glatman, juvenile sadomasochists. And even if they're not committing sex crimes at a young age, they're thinking about them.

Other Common Factors

But even a psychopath with unusual sexual appetites won't necessarily become a serial killer. He might find a partner (or more likely, partners) to cater to his tastes, or he might visit prostitutes who will do the same for a price. He may turn his talents towards becoming a 'love 'em and leave 'em' pick-up artist.

No, something else needs to happen to push our young psychopath over the threshold. An additional X-factor, or factors, needs to be in place. Thanks to the work done by the FBI in interviews with captured serial murderers, we know what some of those factors are.

Born Bad

The idea that someone might be inherently evil would have been scoffed at not too long ago. However, as we begin to understand more about the unique reality that murderers inhabit, it becomes clear that their warped view of the world takes root at an early age.

"Trash Bag Killer" Patrick Kearney said that he knew from age 8 that he would kill people; Ed Kemper had a crush on his second-grade teacher, but told a friend, "If I kiss her I would have to kill her first"; Ted Bundy was leaving butcher's knives in his aunt's bed at the age of just 3; John Joubert was slashing girls with a razor blade before he reached his teens; Harvey Glatman was practicing sadomasochism when he was only 4 years old.

Child Abuse

Not every abused child becomes a serial killer, but a disproportionately high number of serial killers suffered abuse as children. "Boston Strangler," Albert De Salvo's father was a particularly brutal man who regularly beat his wife and children with metal pipes, brought prostitutes home, and even sold his children into slavery. Joseph Kallinger's mother forced him to hold his hand over a flame and beat him if he cried. Henry Lee Lucas' mother beat him so hard she fractured his skull. She also forced the young boy to watch her having sex with men.

And yet, other serial killers grew up in seemingly normal homes - Jeffrey Dahmer, for example, or Joel Rifkin, or Patrick Kearney. Some, like "Pied Piper of Tucson," Charles Schmid, were even pampered and indulged, their every desire catered to.

Domineering Mothers

Many serial killers seem to come from a home with an absent or passive father figure, and a dominating mother. This was certainly the case with both Henry Lee Lucas and Ed Kemper, both of whom eventually murdered their mothers.

Joseph Kallinger's mother was a sadist; Ed Gein's a religious nut who constantly warned him of the dangers of sex. Bobby Joe Long's mother made him sleep in her bed until he was thirteen. Ed

Kemper's mom locked him in the cellar because she said his large size frightened his sisters. Charles Manson's mother reportedly traded him for a pitcher of beer. And at the other end of the scale was "Hillside Strangler" Kenneth Bianchi's cloyingly overprotective mom.

Either way, dysfunctional mother/son relationships seem to be present in the upbringing of an alarmingly high number of serial killers.

Adoption

Millions of children are adopted every year and grow up to live normal, productive lives. However, there are an unusually high percentage of serial killers who were given up by their birth mothers for adoption. David Berkowitz, Charles Schmid, Joel Rifkin, Kenneth Bianchi, and Joseph Kallinger (to name a few) all fall into this category.

Finding out that one was adopted can be devastating for any child, creating a sense of disconnect, an uncertainty over one's identity. And, in a child already suffering from other issues (such as some of those mentioned above), it can be particularly devastating, unleashing feelings of rejection and simmering anger.

Exposure To Violence

Some serial killers blame juvenile exposure to violence for their misdeeds. Ed Gein, for example, claimed that seeing farm animals slaughtered gave him perverted ideas, while both Albert Fish and Andrei Chikatilo blamed their brutal murders on frightening stories they were told as children. As a child, John George Haigh saw a man decapitated by a bomb during the London Blitz in WWII. Richard Ramirez was only thirteen when his cousin committed a murder right in front of him (those who knew him at the time said he showed no emotion and continued to idolize his cousin).

Rejection by Peers

Many serial killers are outsiders and loners in childhood. The nerdy Joel Rifkin was picked on and bullied throughout his school years. Likewise, the diminutive and sickly Patrick Kearney. Henry Lee Lucas was ridiculed and ostracized because of his glass eye, Kenneth Bianchi because of his incontinence. Jeffrey Dahmer was deliberately antisocial as a kid, a teenage alcoholic who laughed when he saw a classmate injured. Harvey Glatman preferred spending time alone in his room indulging in autoerotic strangulation.

Separated from their peers, these troubled youngsters begin to rely on fantasy to bridge the gap. Often these begin as "revenge fantasies" against those who have wronged them, like abusive parents or schoolyard bullies. The relief that these fantasies bring, leads to ever more violent daydreams, which may begin to manifest through two of the three "triad" behaviors, fire-starting and animal cruelty.

Fantasy

The role of fantasy in the metamorphosis of a killer has been extensively studied. All of us fantasize at some time, perhaps about asking a pretty girl out, or meeting our favorite celebrity, or turning out for our favorite sports teams. The fantasies of a fledgling serial killer, though, are a deep and disturbing mix of murder, mutilation, and aberrant sex.

Serial killers will dwell on these fantasies (sometimes for years), deepening them and adding layers of detail. Eventually, though, the fantasy will no longer be enough, and they'll feel compelled to act, the pressure building until it is impossible to resist.

How long before fantasy manifests in reality? Peter Kurten, Jesse Pomeroy, and Mary Bell committed multiple murders as children, Yosemite killer, Cary Stayner, said that he'd fantasized about killing a woman for 30 years before he eventually followed through.

Brain Damage

Brain damage, especially to the hypothalamus, limbic region, and temporal lobe can cause severe behavioral changes, specifically as regards emotion, empathy, and aggression responses.

Many serial killers - Leonard Lake, David Berkowitz, Kenneth Bianchi, John Wayne Gacy, Carl Panzram, Henry Lee Lucas, Bobby Joe Long, among them - have suffered head injuries, either in accidents or in childhood beatings.

Others, Ted Bundy for example, have been subjected to extensive X-rays and brain scans, which revealed no evidence of brain damage or trauma. Neither does everyone who suffers head trauma become a killer. So while brain damage or dysfunction is undoubtedly a factor in the behavior of some serial killers, it is far from being a universal "kill switch."

Societal Influences

Psychopaths find it difficult to accept responsibility for their actions, so it is not surprising that many serial killers blame society for their acts. The poster boy for this theory is Ted Bundy. Bundy has spoken at length about the influence of violent pornography on the killer that he became.

Is there any validity to his claims?

We do seem to be a society that glorifies violence, from live footage of bombs falling on Baghdad to movies in which the hero is every bit as violent as the bad guy he's trying to defeat. Porn, too, is easily available, both online and in movies and magazines. But neither of these provides a rationale for serial murder. If everyone who watched a Rambo movie or downloaded porn was to become a serial killer, we'd have an epidemic on our hands.

Conclusion

At the beginning of the article, I asked, "What makes a serial killer?" The reasons may be more complex than we think, perhaps beyond our comprehension. A better question to ask may be, "Is anyone capable of serial murder?" And the answer to that is an emphatic "No!"

The creation of a serial killer requires a perfect (or more appropriately, an imperfect) storm, whereby some of the factors mentioned above, and perhaps some others that are not, are blended into a toxic brew with psychopathy and sexual deviance.

A combination of aberrant psychology, childhood abuse, and peer rejection leading to the development of fantasies that involve death and sex and then manifest in fire-starting and animal cruelty can hardly fail to produce someone who, given the opportunity, will kill and kill again.

For more True Crime books by Robert Keller please visit

http://bit.ly/kellerbooks

Printed in Great Britain
by Amazon